Insightful Data Visualization with SAS® Viya®

Falko Schulz
Travis Murphy

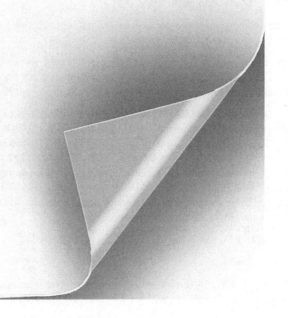

sas.com/books

Contents

About This Book

What Does This Book Cover?

A data visualization is the gateway to artificial intelligence (AI) and big data. A data visualization is a data application answering a question or range or questions for the business user and analyst. It can be a portal or a headline. It is the flexible "on ramp" to data-driven decision making in the enterprise.

SAS has been creating dashboards and data visualizations via many software tools over many decades. This book shows how the latest SAS Viya tools can be used to create data visualizations in an easier, smarter, and more engaging way than ever before. SAS Visual Analytics combined with human creativity can produce endless possibilities. In this book, you will learn tips and techniques for getting the most from your SAS Visual Analytics investment. From beginner to advanced SAS users, this book has something for everyone. Use AI wizards to create data visualization automatically, learn to use advanced analytics in your dashboards to surface smarter insights, and learn to extend SAS Visual Analytics with advanced integrations and options.

People often ask us to show how we build our data visualizations, and this book is a way to share that with the world.

Topics covered in this book include:

- SAS Visual Analytics
- Data visualization with SAS
- Reports and dashboards
- SAS code examples
- Self-service analytics
- Create reports with SAS
- SAS data Access
- Extending SAS beyond drag and drop

Is This Book for You?

This book is for all SAS users.

This book is structured in two parts. First, we step through some foundations and explore ideas about what approaches you can take to create more insightful data visualization. Part two is a practical exploration of achieving these designs with SAS Visual Analytics on SAS Viya. If you are interested in understanding more about dashboards, each part has something for you.

If you are an intermediate or advanced SAS user, then this book will assist you in understanding the value of creating for the audience using impactful visualization, and the possibilities that visualizations provide for engaging your audience.

For a beginner SAS user, this book provides the necessary overview to understand dashboard and report foundations and their origins to then progress through the book and use the step-by-step examples to work along with.

This book is aimed at SAS users who create and design reports and dashboards for their users. Managers can use this book to determine what their teams could create and design with SAS® Visual Analytics.

All levels of SAS skills are covered in this book: beginners, intermediate, and advanced. Beginners learns to use SAS to add data and create dashboards with ease, intermediate users get to extend with custom data elements and custom visual elements, and advanced users get to see the power of code and APIs to enhance and share data visualizations.

Prerequisites

You do not have to have any previous experience with SAS tools to read this book. However, if you do have some experience with SAS code and data preparation, then you may find some parts of this book and examples easier.

Examples: Data, Reports, and Code

There are examples provided in this book, including code samples, reports, and data where applicable. These files can be downloaded from the author pages at support.sas.com/Schulz and support.sas.com/Murphy.

Software Used

Support Documentation is located at http://support.sas.com/documentation/

Here are the specific software versions used in this book:

- SAS Visual Analytics 8.5.1
- SAS Visual Statistics 8.5.1
- SAS Visual Data Mining & Machine Learning 8.5
- SAS Data Preparation 8.5

Documentation links and further reading are outlined in this book.

SAS OnDemand for Academics

If you are using SAS OnDemand for Academics to access data and run your programs, then please check the SAS OnDemand for Academics page to ensure that the software contains the product or products that you need to run the code: https://www.sas.com/en_us/software/on-demand-for-academics.html.

Code examples are designed to run against the open data referenced.

SAS Visual Analytics Trial

To access a free trial of SAS Visual Analytics software, go to: www.sas.com/va.

Samples in this book are designed to work with SAS Visual Analytics 8.5.

We Want to Hear from You

SAS Press books are written *by* SAS Users *for* SAS Users. We welcome your participation in their development and your feedback on SAS Press books that you are using. Please visit sas.com/books to do the following:

- Sign up to review a book
- Recommend a topic
- Request information on how to become a SAS Press author
- Provide feedback on a book

Do you have questions about a SAS Press book that you are reading? Contact the author through saspress@sas.com or https://support.sas.com/author_feedback.

SAS has many resources to help you find answers and expand your knowledge. If you need additional help, see our list of resources: sas.com/books.

About These Authors

Travis and Falko get asked all the time to help people with creating engaging data visualization with SAS Visual Analytics. One way to share this to a larger audience is to create a book, and this is that book. In a paper presented at SAS Global Forum 2018, Travis and Falko teamed up to share some insight on creating supercharged dashboards using SAS Visual Analytics. That paper set the foundation for this book idea, and together the two authors aim to combine, create, and share something great to enable the reader to re-create the examples to take their data visualizations to the next level. This book introduces many concepts and provide step-by-step examples and samples to reuse in SAS software around the globe.

 Falko Schulz is widely regarded as one of the best infographic data visualization creators using drag-and-drop tools like SAS Visual Analytics. He is also a distinguished developer in SAS R&D, making SAS Visual Analytics what it is today. His creative approach has produced many stunning visualization examples. Falko has been involved in many projects over the years helping customers to visualize business insights and tell data stories. He is an active SAS community member and is enabling SAS users by sharing technical papers, data visualization examples, and blogs posts to explain and show the capabilities of SAS.

Falko Schulz is a Distinguished Software Developer in the SAS Business Intelligence Research and Development division. He works actively on products such as SAS Visual Analytics, further enhancing user experience and analytical capabilities. Falko has a strong background in delivering business analytical applications in a wide range of industries.

Prior to joining the R&D division, Falko worked in customer-facing roles and was responsible for critical technical implementations and BI architectural designs. During his 20 years at SAS, Falko has worked in various countries including Germany, Australia, and the US.

For more information, visit:

support.sas.com/schulz

Your comments and questions are valued and encouraged. Contact the author at:

LinkedIn: https://www.linkedin.com/in/falkoschulz/

Email: Falko.Schulz@sas.com

 Travis is a strong advocate and evangelist for self-service analytics and data visualization. A data visualization and business intelligence maven, he has helped many organizations deliver on the promise of self-service analytics and get the most from their investment in business analytics software.

Travis Murphy has worked for over 20 years in data warehousing, business intelligence, and analytics. Prior to SAS, Travis held roles with other large IT vendors focused on business analytics products. These roles included product marketing, consulting/implementation, training, and presales. His experience includes working with customers and vendors implementing data solutions.

Within SAS, Travis has held presales, technical account management, business solution management, and marketing roles focused on SAS data visualization tools. Travis is always trying to better communicate the value and insight of data using software tools and get business users and stakeholders more involved in the use of data.

Travis is a published SAS author and has presented at SAS Global Forums, conferences, and SAS marketing roadshows. He continues to evangelize the benefits of approachable analytics and data visualization.

For more information, visit:

support.sas.com/murphy

Your comments and questions are valued and encouraged. Contact the author at:

LinkedIn: https://www.linkedin.com/in/travismmurphy/

Email: Travis.Murphy@sas.com

Acknowledgments

The authors would like to thank the SAS press team of editors, designers, and reviewers for their fantastic support – this book could not and would not exist if it was not for you and your dedication and constant mentoring.

Falko Schulz Acknowledgments

Writing a book is much more difficult and time consuming compared to papers I have written for events like SAS Global Forum. No doubt the year 2020 has been a challenging one for many other reasons as well. However, being able to focus on this project during that time is also very rewarding, and you feel like you accomplished something. You learn so much during the process and get the opportunity to work with so many talented people across the organization. I would like to thank my manager Don Chapman for supporting me during the process and allowing me to dedicate time to work on this project. Also, a big thanks to various people in our organization especially in the R&D division. People were always there to answer questions and to help as needed. A very special thanks to Travis, who not only convinced me writing this book (in a good sense!), but also for the very creative approach in getting our ideas written down. We always wanted to write a full book to cover all aspects around data visualization techniques. The book certainly would not be the same without his help.

Travis Murphy Acknowledgments

I would like to thank my wife, Emily, and sons, William and Edward, for their patience and support through this process as writing a book does take time away from other pursuits. I also want to thank all the great mentors I have had over my career and particularly at SAS. Thanks to SAS Canada and SAS Australia for the great chance to work and learn from so many awesome people. I want to thank my Mum and Dad for teaching me to think big and follow my dreams wherever they take me. Finally, I want to thank my friend and coauthor Falko for agreeing to the book project, for the great collaboration over the years, and I look forward to sharing our combined thoughts and ideas with the world.

Part 1: In Principle

In **Part 1**, we introduce the basic concepts about data visualizations and why they are important. We explore origins, types, and considerations when designing data visualizations. We discuss where SAS can add value to the process of creating dashboards and data visualizations. You will see how to derive additional value from big data and better engage your audience.

Chapter 1: Data-Driven Journeys

Overview

This chapter sets the tone for what is to come in the book and includes some visual examples of data visualizations and what you can expect to create with SAS Viya yourself. Looking back in time, we will discuss how common terminology in data visualization, like the dashboard, came to be and introduce topics that we delve into further as the book continues.

Audience

This chapter is for all readers because it provides an introduction and origins of what is contained in this book on data visualization. No matter your experience is in SAS Viya, you will be shown some ideas to help explain what is to come.

> "Every company has big data in its future, and every company will eventually be in the data business."

Thomas H. Davenport

Introduction

Studies have shown that readers of newspapers skim the paper for headlines, images, and data visualizations to decide if they want to read the article. This skimming is heightened in a world of personalized newsfeeds across many channels and sources. This means that the dashboards of yesterday might not be equipped to meet the audience requirements of today. Learning from other information channels provides some great ideas for data visualization and dashboard design. As the quote from Davenport alludes, all companies will be leveraging big data and will be challenged to turn this into competitive advantage. Just remember that data visualizations are primarily designed to deliver this valuable information with clarity and simplicity... do yours?

Creating modern dashboards and reports that can be shared and remembered by people is so important today. In Figure 1.1 you can see an example of sharing COVID-19 data in a poster format created using SAS Visual Analytics on SAS Viya. This book steps through many examples and tips to make your SAS Visual Analytics reports and dashboards grab your audience's attention and deliver insight with your data visualizations.

Figure 1.1: SAS Visual Analytics example showing the global impact of coronavirus (COVID-19) outbreak for selected countries (Schulz 2020)

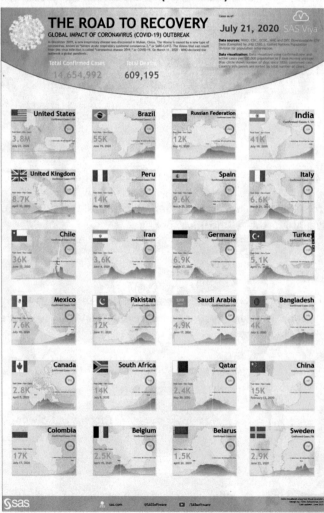

Attracting and retaining the attention of a modern-day audience is tougher than ever before. The rise of information volume and velocity has changed our lives in almost every way. We are in the information age, and we are "informavores" (Miller 1983).

INFORMAVORE:

Information + *Vorare* (Latin – to devour)

Originally used as a way of describing humans in the Information Age, being informavores has quickly become our new way of life. In the way that herbivores eat plants or carnivores eat meat, the informavore consumes information as the primary source of their diet. Today with social media and our digital life, information analysis is much harder than ever before. Using this simple analogy in the idea of a carnivore or omnivore, an informavore is simply a consumer of information. The question is whether your information is cutting through into the stream at all? With so many options today for information, if your data projects are not being consumed, people are filling the gap with other sources.

In short, as analysts, our information products are competing with a massive amount of information today, from social media, to niche websites, Reddit, news (fake included), microblogs, video blogs, and ever-changing sources that we rely on to live our modern lives. To deliver value to our audience, we need to create impactful, data-driven journeys.

This is important for data analysts today because we are crafting the interaction with data for our audience to consume. The audience is overwhelmed with information, yet they need information to survive and function. This dichotomy is the challenge of our time and has seen data visualizations rise in record numbers to bridge this gap and make information more consumable. To break into the audience's trusted network of information, analysts need to create impact with their information products, especially data dashboards.

Dashboards

A common type of data project that sets the foundation for modern data visualization is a dashboard. People often start the history of data visualization with hieroglyphs or cave paintings; however, more recently with big data transformation, the origins are more consistent with business intelligence software tools and dashboards. The origins of the dashboard from the practical and literal to the modern use as a form of interface to data science, the term has had a journey well before this book was written. The following definitions are useful to understand a dashboard and decide what this means for the modern analyst. Webster's definitions are great to get the essence of the word dashboard as there is some history here.

A dashboard was:

"a screen on the front of a usually horse-drawn vehicle to intercept water, mud, or snow"

Or as time marched on:

"a panel extending across the interior of a vehicle
(such as an automobile) below the windshield and
usually containing instruments and controls"

(Merriam-Webster)

The origin of the word dashboard is interesting and sits at the heart of technical advancement but is also a continued nod to the past. Originally used to describe a horse-drawn carriage's kick board, the dashboard was used to keep drivers safe and stop mud and dirt from hitting them. This term evolved over time and was continued to be used as the modern carriages with motors came into use like the automobile and other instrumentation. This instrumentation shows the performance of the vehicle in real time and over time – with very narrow parameters.

The modern use of the word dashboard harkens back to that era, and now we travel the world each minute on our smart devices and the internet. As was true in the past, a dashboard protected the user from the dirt and mud of what was being kicked up, which still holds true for data visualization today. Let's take a look at what a modern data dashboard is:

"a dashboard is a user interface that, somewhat
resembling an automobile's dashboard, organizes and
presents information in a way that is easy to read.
However, a computer dashboard is more likely to be
interactive than an automobile dashboard."

(Whatis.com)

The modern dashboard keeps this principle and extends it to vast nuance of data and meaning. Now the dashboard can show data and performance of a single item, a collection of items on a single topic, or even a collection of items on many topics – every time this modern dashboard can differ. Dashboards are both a collection of data visualizations and can also perform as a single infographic data visualization. Businesses across the globe rely on dashboards to support their digital transformation. The modern dashboard has become a data application almost like an app on your phone. Just like apps, you can have useful and not so useful dashboards. The not so useful dashboards are easily forgotten and have limited reason for the audience to come back. We have all seen dashboards that make you excited and ones that make you sigh.

Engaging the audience each time a new modern dashboard is created can be tough and often gets lost in the noise of the rest of life's modern information requirements. Today, people are informavores, and this means they don't waste time learning something with perceived low value.

A Dashboard Supports Decision Making

A dashboard, like the original cockpit-style display, is a collection of information served visually to assist with "just in time" decision making. This has shifted during the digital age, and during the automation age, and it continues to evolve and will keep evolving in the AI era to come. What was a car dashboard of simple gauges and levers in the past has changed to a more nuanced and dynamic context-sensitive layered display with many more areas of data and information. No longer do we have to look down at a gauge as a heads-up display (HUD) allows augmented reality to provide the most important information in our main view. In an aircraft scenario, the cockpit has evolved also in a similar way. Think of it like this: the automation increased, and the human now has different requirements of the dashboard or data visualization. The data-driven organization is also heavily evolving and information is everywhere, leaving people wondering – what do I look at?

You could call this information overload, and as the data increases, the dashboard concept has been embedded in nearly every digital channel that we have today – even refrigerators have dashboard displays letting us know updates such as: the milk is running low, the balance of cold air is correct in all chambers, and the vegetables and meat are still fresh. The audience is getting quite adept at understanding useful and not so useful information displays in today's generation. Simply put, humans are becoming great users of technology. The issue is that many of us are not great creators of technology, just great users of the technology. The smart phone generation has seen everything become a dashboard showing many notifications like the number of messages in their inbox, the number of tasks on the to-do list today, and when someone *likes* their social media post.

The great evolution of a dashboard has required data visualization tools to evolve and to become simpler than ever before. We now require simplicity *and* the flexibility to keep all the data-driven journey requirements covered. The boardroom needs information at the speed of thought, and this book shows you how to create modern dashboards and data visualizations that can be shared and dynamically explored by your teams using SAS Visual Analytics on SAS Viya. Enhance your existing dashboards and reports with easy drag-and-drop wizards while still providing performance, repeatability, and scalability on massive data that your enterprise demands.

Foundations of a Modern Dashboard

As introduced above, a great dashboard has some simple characteristics. Here are some ideas about what works for users of dashboards and why they work.

Intended Audience

Dashboards and reports need to support actions, not just share insights from the data. Choosing the right dashboard type for your audience ensures you provide the correct format and options to support your audience.

Figure 1.2: Types of dashboards should match your audience requirements

To achieve your next project, you should think of dashboards as belonging to four possible categories. As seen in Figure 1.2, the four categories are:

1. Operational – the "now" aspect of the business – for example, the performance on the factory floor or the call center operations.
2. Strategic – KPI performance and future projections.
3. Analytical – artificial intelligence (AI) and machine-learning (ML) rich dashboards.
4. Tactical – monitor details within an organization against the strategies.

These categories provide some excellent guard rails for your dashboard and report designs and how the audience will use the dashboard. Then you can also think of other information products that may be a better fit for that category including reports or notifications. Often, the category is also an indicator of the audience, but this is not always the case. If you overlay author Stephen Few's thoughts on dashboards, then you could also create common subcategories of audience and break them down again to management and reporting dashboards (Few 2006). Although, this may not be necessary as the target audience is often clear by the category. From experience, though, each category above requires a collection of information products like dashboards, reports, and alerts to harden the production processes needed to provide robust services to your stakeholders. We could do an entire book on these categories alone and include these to ensure you can see where your next dashboard project fits, as this will provide initial guidance on how your dashboard may be used and by whom.

What dictates the final dashboard is the intended audience and their skill levels with data. A dashboard is an information application, and like many of the best apps, the best dashboards don't require any additional training or special skills to use. The user can simply open the dashboard and start to navigate by clicking and moving on areas that matter or are interesting to the question the audience has. Today, all insight from data is competing for a user's attention, and we only have seconds to provide a reason for the audience to stay. A great dashboard needs to grab the attention of the audience.

A Thoughtful, Data-Driven Journey

Crafting a deliberate and simple story line throughout the data-driven journey is important. The best dashboards or data visualization engage the audience on multiple levels. This is achieved with the following considerations.

- Layered Context. The best dashboards are layered, and these layers are often built into multiple tabs or pages of your dashboard and linked together to move between these layers with context from each question the audience has. The challenge today is cutting through the noise and grabbing the attention of the audience to drive more engagement with your dashboard designs.

- Intuitive and Simple Pathways. How will the audience navigate the dashboard? Will they click or tap the tabs or each object? What path will they take? Is there a single line of thought navigation built in, or are there multiple pathways to take for the user at any time? Actionable insight is key for a dashboard user, and each click of the mouse or tap of the screen should provide more detail or a different perspective, while still maintaining context. The dashboard moves from highlights to detail with ease and simplicity.

- Interactive. It is important to consider how interactive or static the dashboard needs to be, and sometimes this is not for the designer to decide, but rather consider how the users will interact with the final design. Static dashboards are more like today's infographics as they will often end up on a wall as a poster, on a television screen in the lobby, or as a social media tile shared on the internet.

Design Once and Use Everywhere

A great data visualization is designed once and used by many users in many contexts. This means that there need to be multiple hooks and entry points into the dashboard or data visualization. Each user gets a custom experience even though the look and feel are never different, so the context is the only thing that changes. Creating a context-sensitive landing page for your data-driven journey allows for many entry points to the same content and increases the use cases and audience without limiting the value for each group. Delivering enterprise-ready data visualization requires resources to be shared, and this is true with the outputs of data visualization projects. We will explore some of these key considerations in more detail throughout this book and highlight when these are leveraged in each data visualization example in the upcoming chapters.

Creating Data Visualizations

Data visualizations are like an iceberg – they look simple and approachable above water; however, much lies beneath the surface to ensure they make sense, are accurate, and trustworthy. A plethora of software tools claim they create data visualization and dashboards today. In recent years, we have seen the growth and consolidation in vendors in this space, and a heightened claim of advanced capability of tools and broader platforms. It is important to look at data visualizations from two perspectives, the **analyst** and the **audience**. These software tools have strengths and weaknesses, and this book will highlight how SAS Visual Analytics provides many features to complement other SAS solutions, but in particular how the analyst and the audience interact in design and use of data visualizations.

The world is full of hype around AI, and many software vendors claim to embed it and enable businesses to achieve success. In reality, the hype falls short when reviewing capabilities in more detail across these solutions. The steps toward robots and the science fiction view of AI have to start somewhere, and this is important for the future applications. One of the most impactful uses of AI to business users is embedded AI, which assists both analytics professionals and novices alike and is changing the game when it comes to data visualization and communicating insight. SAS provides advanced capabilities to users of all levels via a visual interface and code. These can be combined to deliver the most impactful data visualizations that you have ever achieved. SAS has made advancement in embedding AI and ML into the tools that also create and share data visualizations, making SAS the premier platform or engine for your organization's information. The dashboard of today should be as easy as PowerPoint and as smart as AI. Your analytics platform needs to enable you to have flexibility and simplicity to achieve simple analysis and the most complex AI. Here are some attributes of the platform that are useful to consider, and this book will aim to unlock these throughout:

- Easy to get data in and scalable for complex processes
- Easy to get insight and flexible to add precise visuals
- Easy to share and embed anywhere
- Simple for individuals and ready for enterprise
- Drag-and-drop or code where needed

With over 40 years' experience in data analysis and enterprise deployment, SAS has all the components and personas covered to support any organization. Data-driven journeys have been a continuous focus for SAS since the beginning. SAS has been excellent at seeing and adapting to those market shifts in technology and the latest trends. SAS Visual Analytics continues to evolve and include new capabilities to tell amazing data stories and create data visualization. SAS Visual Analytics includes built-in intelligence and drag-and-drop wizards to create insightful, data-driven journeys with great visual appeal.

Data Visualization Gallery

No matter the skills that you have today, you can create data visualizations with SAS. You can either be a consumer of information, or a creator of information, or a combination of both depending on your area of expertise. This book shows you that you have an option, right now, with your current SAS investment. You can step forward with your data-driven journey by applying a makeover to existing reports and dashboards or by taking some of the characteristics of the examples in this book and applying these in the build phase of your next data visualization project.

Let us begin with showing what you will be able to achieve by the end of this book with some visual examples. Here is a gallery of the type of data visualizations that you will create by the end of this book.

Figure 1.3: Sample dashboard created with SAS Visual Analytics showing data visualization embedded in a highly formatted image of a desktop (Schulz 2018a)

Figure 1.4: Sample dashboard created with SAS Visual Analytics comparing 2012 and 2016 NASA nighttime satellite images to illustrate how illumination patterns have changed over time (Schulz 2018b)

Figure 1.5: Sample dashboard created with SAS Visual Analytics displaying forest fire data from 1992–2015 in the United States showing the locations, common causes, and when wildfires occur (Schulz 2018c)

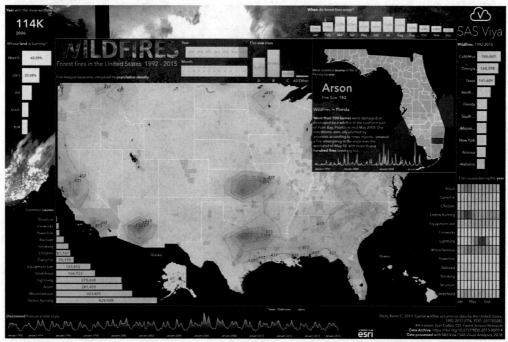

Figure 1.6: Sample dashboard created with SAS Visual Analytics showing public pest data to create an operational dashboard to monitor rodent and pests in New York City (NYC) (Schulz 2018d)

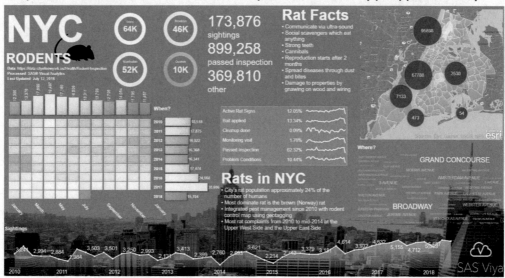

Figure 1.7: Sample dashboard created with SAS Visual Analytics showing meteorite impacts across the globe from 2500BC to 2012 and colored by impact type (Schulz 2018e)

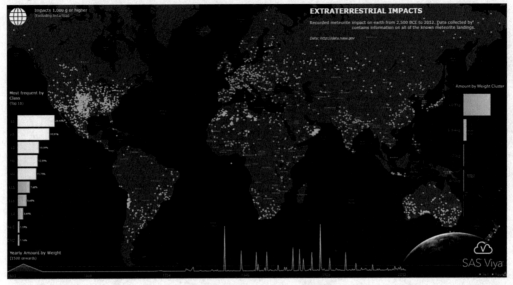

Figure 1.8: Sample dashboard created with SAS Visual Analytics visualizing customer segmentation using analytical clustering and location analytics (Schulz 2017a)

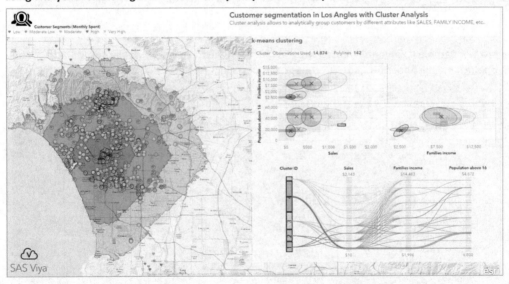

Figure 1.9: Sample dashboard created with SAS Visual Analytics showing ticket member distribution based on geographical location and ticket sales (Schulz 2018f)

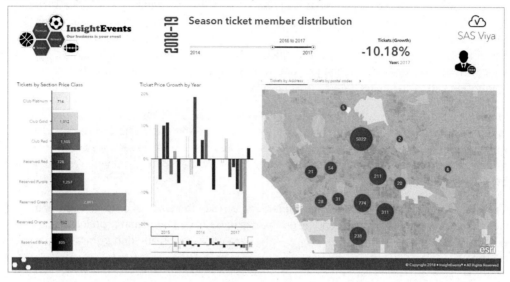

Figure 1.10: Sample dashboard created with SAS Visual Analytics displaying flight delays including a map highlighting major hubs at risk of delay, including indicators for best and worst airports (Schulz 2017b)

Conclusion

This book looks at how the recent releases of SAS Visual Analytics running on SAS Viya allows analysts to design and create visually rich and impactful dashboards and data visualizations like never before. You will learn tips and techniques to get the most from your SAS Visual Analytics software, which you can apply back at the office and with your team. You will be shown the perfect balance of creative ideas and practical examples to better engage your entire organization with high impact data driven journeys.

We will cover some topics to set the stage and break down why impact matters in your dashboards. Then we will step through a gallery of examples and discuss how to re-create your own at your organization. You can easily follow along and download the samples and work through each exercise. Also, you can pick up some tricks and tips to help you with creating your next data visualization.

As per the example visualizations shown earlier, you can see the types of outputs you will be able to create, and these may be building on the dashboards that you create today. Or you may get some ideas on how to makeover your existing data visualization and find inspiration for your next project.

References

"Dashboard." Merriam-Webster.com Dictionary, s.v. Accessed September 1, 2020, https://www.merriam-webster.com/dictionary/dashboard.

"Informavore Definition." World Wide Words. Available http://www.worldwidewords.org/turnsofphrase/tp-inf3.htm. Accessed on February 26, 2020.

Davenport, Thomas H. 2014. *Big Data at Work: Dispelling the Myths, Uncovering the Opportunities*. Boston: Harvard Business Review Press.

Few, Stephen. 2006. *Information Dashboard Design: The Effective Visual Communication of Data*. Sebastopol, CA: O'Reilly.

Machlup, Fritz and Una Mansfield. 1983. *The Study of Information: Interdisciplinary Messages*. New York, NY: John Wiley and Sons Inc.

Rouse, Margaret. n.d. "What Is a Dashboard?" WhatIs.com, Last updated September 2005. Accessed February 20, 2020. http://searchcio.techtarget.com/definition/dashboard.

Schulz, Falko. 2017a. "Customer Segmentation with Cluster Analysis." SAS Communities. August 6, 2017. https://communities.sas.com/t5/SAS-Visual-Analytics-Gallery/Customer-segmentation-with-Cluster-Analysis/ta-p/482350.

Schulz, Falko. 2017b. "Flight cancellations and delays in the United States." *SAS Communities*. August 3, 2017. https://communities.sas.com/t5/SAS-Visual-Analytics-Gallery/Flight-cancellations-and-delays-in-the-United-States/ta-p/482348.

Schulz, Falko. 2018a. "Global airports - connecting the world." *SAS Communities*. August 29, 2018. https://communities.sas.com/t5/SAS-Visual-Analytics-Gallery/Global-airports-connecting-the-world/ta-p/488388.

Schulz, Falko. 2018b. "The dark side: analyzing global changes in nighttime illumination." *SAS Communities*. July 9, 2018. https://communities.sas.com/t5/SAS-Visual-Analytics-Gallery/The-dark-side-analyzing-global-changes-in-nighttime-illumination/ta-p/468253.

Schulz, Falko. 2018c. "Analyzing US Wildfires using SAS Visual Analytics." *SAS Communities*. June 7, 2018. https://communities.sas.com/t5/SAS-Visual-Analytics-Gallery/Analyzing-US-Wildfires-using-SAS-Visual-Analytics/ta-p/467894.

Schulz, Falko. 2018d. "New York City - Rodent Inspection." *SAS Communities*. July 13, 2018.
https://communities.sas.com/t5/SAS-Visual-Analytics-Gallery/New-York-City-Rodent-Inspection/ta-p/477334.

Schulz, Falko. 2018e. "Extraterrestrial Impacts - Recorded meteorite impacts on earth." *SAS Communities*. August 15,
2018. https://communities.sas.com/t5/SAS-Visual-Analytics-Gallery/Extraterrestrial-Impacts-Recorded-meteorite-
impacts-on-earth/ta-p/482358.

Schulz, Falko. 2018f. "Analyze ticket sales using location analytics and customer segmentation in SAS® Visual Analytics."
SAS Communities. April 26, 2018. https://blogs.sas.com/content/sascom/2018/04/26/analyze-ticket-sales-using-
location-analytics-and-customer-segmentation-in-sas-visual-analytics/.

Chapter 2: Three Is of Visualization Value – INFORM, INSIGHT, INSPIRE

Overview

The goal of an analytics platform is to create the shortest path from data to decision, and this could be in many forms, including data visualizations, which are created from a vast volume of data in your organization. This chapter provides an overview of a proposed way to think about the information flow from raw data to useful information. We look at this from two persona perspectives: the analyst creating insight and the audience consuming insight.

Audience

This chapter is aimed at all SAS users because it outlines a way to think about the different persona perspectives without talking about the SAS technology.

"Innovation requires articulation."

Walter Isaacson

Introduction

Looking at business processes from different perspectives is a useful way to challenge and understand possible relationships that are not instantly obvious. When first looking at this book idea, we thought a potential benefit to readers would be to look at this process from both the audience perspective and the analyst perspective. In the quote introducing this chapter, Isaacson is trying to highlight that to ensure that innovation becomes a reality, you need to be a story teller. This was in reference to Grace Hopper and the programming of early computers: the ideas only became reality due to the talent of the innovator who used deft storytelling skills to show the value of the computer in language that non-technical audiences can also understand (Isaacson 2014).

Almost all innovation for modern enterprises starts and ends with data, and the innovator must tell a clear story to drive ideas forward. All processes can be analyzed when you find a common element, and the common element that we found here was effort or skills needed today to perform the process from each role's point of view. Today, there is a focus on the skills gap in data science and AI, and as we expect these requirements to grow in the future, it is interesting to look at the skills needed.

This book focuses on the importance of data visualization, which has been redefined by human information consumption and the increased reliance on data-driven insights. There is a documented gap in data science and STEM skills, which is forecast by analysts to increase if we don't prepare for digital disruption across many industries (Insidebigdata 2018). The benefit of selecting a platform like SAS is the ability to build institutional skills with a consistent user experience and software to match the user's ability and allow a pathway for skills growth as they develop and require more control over their analytics.

The spectrum of skills to create impactful data journeys can be seen from the two roles: analyst and audience. This is explored further in this chapter. However, our proposition also layers in another perspective: how much actionable information can be gleaned from the data interactions along this data journey? Think of this as a Visualization Value scale.

Now that we have started to think about the roles in dashboard processes, the skills needed, and how effective the value is from the dashboard, let us use a model to link these together: introducing the **"Three Is of Visualization Value."**

The Three Is of Visualization Value

Overview of a Model

It is useful to think of a visualization through two lenses: inputs and outputs. Also consider visualizations by distinct persona: the analyst and the audience. The analyst's goals are to gain answers quickly, and this is often done once or in their own single user session or project. The audience prefers information at a glance that is relevant and context-rich. The audience and analyst have the same goal; however, there are some barriers preventing both from getting what they want. Clearly, human effort is common for both. This could be illustrated by inverse processes: analyst effort and audience effort. This can be seen in Figure 2.1 with both roles highlighted. Before we get too far, let's talk about the value within a data visualization.

Figure 2.1: The Three Is of Visualization Value – analyst needs to work hard to allow the audience to work less

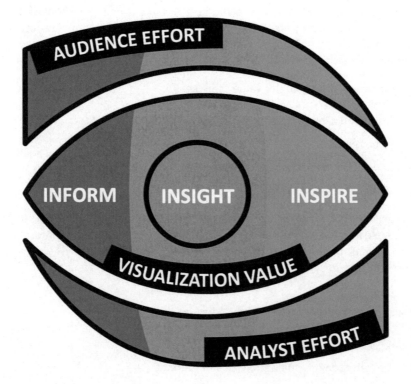

The Visualization Value Scale

It is useful to think of a dashboard on a value scale, and the diagram in Figure 2.1 shows this from left to right. The visualization value is often limited by the software features, the skills of the analyst, and the skills of the audience. The three value stages used in this model are the three Is, so a visualization can: INFORM, provide INSIGHT, or INSPIRE.

Inform: Get an answer and move on quickly. "To acquaint (oneself) with knowledge of a subject." Accessing information is relatively easy effort for the analyst, but the audience must work harder to get the value that they need from the dashboard. More effort is required from the audience to get the value they need if they access the outputs from the analyst during the INFORM stage.

Some examples of actions and outputs in this value stage are:

- Formatted spreadsheet with some initial summary tables
- Summary data extract provided from a source system

- Raw data for further use
- Summary data
- Single number emailed to answer single question

Insight: Leverage artificial intelligence (AI) and analytics to gain more from the dashboard. This value level uncovers previously unknown patterns and linkages in data, which can only occur when using advanced analytics and AI. Both audience and analyst have to put in effort to see the value from these additional machine learning (ML) concepts and the value that they provide.

Some examples of actions and outputs in this value stage are:

- Interactive dashboard allowing filter and data subsets
- Static production reports
- Analytically driven wizards and embedded AI
- Exploration without additional formatting

Inspire: Share a compelling story supported with data that includes heavy formatting and styling. You have created a simple interface to the value in the data that cuts through all the information noise. The audience has a fast understanding of the visualization because the analyst worked hard to INSPIRE their audience to act. The audience wants to return and interact again with this data visualization.

Some examples of actions and outputs in this value stage are:

- Infofragment – a small factoid data visualization
- Infographic – a collection of visualizations in story format
- Dashboard – a data application that is highly interactive and formatted
- Printed poster – a collection of infographics for story telling offline
- Conversations – data visualization used to support a natural language interaction

As the requirement to present data and tell stories increases across businesses globally, we can see SAS being used more as a collaboration and presentation suite. Not every visualization needs to inspire, rather it needs to be fit for your audience. If the analyst is also the audience, then you might be happy to INFORM only and proceed to your next task of the day. However, if *you* are not the audience, who is *your* audience? The analyst needs to build the dashboard to the value required for the audience. The Three-I model works on a simple premise, that the skills required to create and leverage data visualization with high value are varied. You often see this when looking at the members involved in data teams in an organization. Data science is a team sport for a reason. The analyst is very good at finding the answer within a world of data; however, the challenge can be to create an engaging story to make that data actionable by the business decision maker. Similarly, the best storyteller with data can sometimes not have the depth of skills to reach right into the data to support or create that story. There are exceptions and this model caters for that because these skills could belong to one person or be spread across multiple people.

The *audience* and the *analyst* generally have different skills and often different needs for information. The challenge of the analyst is to create the most engaging self-service or automated interactions with the data for their audience. Therefore, we need to know our audience to build high-value data visualizations. The challenge for software tools is to simplify and automate these data journeys for all users. SAS Visual Analytics provides great options to support analysts and audiences for all organizations. Skills to achieve each level of actionable information varies from task to task and software tool to software tool. The next section attempts to break these skills down and provide some structure to understand how each role can grow their skills to achieve more from their use of data.

The Personas

Data visualizations and dashboards are not the only IT project that needs to think of the audience before delivering the product. Dashboards and data visualizations can look like a data application, providing an audience with the required user experience to solve a business problem. User experience is more than just for software developers in the modern world, it is for an analyst also.

We see this user experience in so many aspects of modern life, for example, online shopping websites where the user experience with data is absolutely critical. The website might have two suggested items based on data analysis, and you see this represented to the audience as a picture or collection of pictures. However, underneath, the AI is being used to analyze the data for this outcome. The programmer of the website could have stopped at the point where they had the fit statistic of the model and said "find your own products" or even generated a ranked list of products in a tabular format with every product SKU available listed and sorted by fit statistic. The developer could take this a step further and display top 10 products in a list and let the audience decide. This does not always get the desired outcome until you overlay additional elements and data points like product image, user ratings, and special sale pricing, which the AI can tune to your tastes and preferences. As this example tries to highlight, we all have options as analysts to pass the outputs to the audience with less effort for the audience.

Data visualization is everywhere and embedded in so many interactions in daily life that our audience expects to get high-quality data interactions. A graph is not the only output to communicate insight, and knowing what the audience truly desires is the key to creating high-value interactions.

Let's step through each of these two roles in more detail.

The Analyst

The skill required of an analyst is simply to get some information from the data. However, the analyst needs to know ML and AI options within a toolset to get some insight that enriches the existing data. ML and AI provide additional insight because of the math, not just the analyst knowledge of the data structure or business problem.

The analyst needs to understand a tool's capability intimately to create impact from its analysis, and a large part of this is having an empathy and understanding of downstream users. Sometimes there is no clear right or wrong decision here as the analyst will create outputs for their own use! It is interesting as we add the audience into the model. The audience is often a different person or group in an organization who can vary in profile from the analyst.

Who Is the Analyst?

If dashboards were easy, we don't need any drag-and-drop tools for the analyst, and we could just code it all, right? Not quite. It is important to take a moment to explore the broad requirements for an analyst. The following are a list of analyst personas who need to have various code, low-code, and no-code options in tools today:

- Developer/Programmer – comfortable with code and programming with or without data
- Data Scientist – comfortable with code and data analysis languages and a focus on ML
- Citizen Data Scientist – have studied statistics and often are deep in applying analytics to business problems – some prefer code, others prefer drag-and-drop tools
- Business Analyst – mostly skilled in linking data outcomes to business outcomes
- Power Consumer – consume information and comfortable interacting with data visualizations including changing data and applying filters

Figure 2.2: The Three Is of Visualization Value – analyst effort and steps

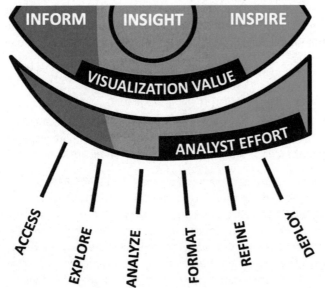

Analyst Effort

No matter the tools that they choose to solve their challenges, the analyst must apply their skills in various stages. Within the analyst's data journey there are necessary steps to realize the value from data, as seen in Figure 2.2. The following steps are regularly conducted during their data visualization project:

1. Access – accessing the data from the source systems is a common part of all dashboard and data visualization projects and presents various challenges ranging from size of data, location, access, quality, and trust.

2. Explore – Once the data is available, the analyst needs to explore the data. This can be achieved with many approaches like simple queries to an entire profile of the data set. This provides understanding of the complete data set and possible topics and opportunity to get answers from the data.

3. Analyze – at this step, the analyst is leveraging the available self-service analytics to uncover relationships and patterns in the data set. Applying AI to the data adds a lot of value to the analyst; however, it might require some understanding of the analytical models or methods being used.

4. Format – general formatting is within most analyst's skills and is essential to tie the insight together for the audience sharing.

5. Refine – make necessary formatting enhancements to resonate with the selected audience.

6. Deploy – share the data visualization with the audience in their preferred channel and format. This is so important to ensure the consumption and reliance on the data visualization.

Technology skill set and subject area expertise often determines how capable the same person is at each step. Recently, the rise in solutions for this persona have meant that keeping up with skills requires analysts to be more technical. An outcome of this skills shift has meant that there is even more emphasis on creating simple interfaces than ever before as mastering complex code is prohibitive for many audiences.

The Audience

The audience requirements are varied across any data visualization project. Often, success of these projects relies on whether the audience engages with the dashboard or data visualization. So, getting the audience requirements clearly identified from the beginning are critical.

If the audience only gets presented output that the analyst created at the **INFORM** stage, they need a high level of skill to understand and use that output for their own decisions. When the audience gets outputs from the **INSIGHT** stage from the analyst, they need to understand how to read outputs from AI and ML. This is possible with education, but it can be overwhelming initially and might require support to interpret the visualizations. The **INSPIRE** stage is where the analyst has created a relevant and impressive visualization that the audience can process and act on without any additional skills. This stage is the ultimate in creating memorable and engaging data journeys that keep the audience wanting more. Knowing your audience requirements will determine the value your visualization should deliver.

Who Is Your Audience?

To understand your audience, it is important to explore the personas. The following list of personas is not exhaustive; however, it does provide some considerations on the requirements of these users and the capabilities that they need in their dashboards or data visualization. Audience personas are interesting and really fall within a spectrum of data literacy and data skills. On one hand, we have business teams and line of business (LOB), who might be highly skilled in business expertise, yet struggle with the skills required to sort through the noise. On the other end of the spectrum, we have data teams who also need access to AI- and ML-driven data visualization to support their own team needs to interpret and share outcomes from advanced analytics.

The following is a list of profiles who make up most audiences today as well as the capabilities they need their dashboards to have:

- Casual Consumer – actionable insight for instant consumption and action
- Executive and Board Members – clarity and trust for decision support
- LOB/Business Team Member – some interactivity and repeatability to assist regular business functions
- Business Analyst – structured entry point and flexibility to create their own data journey
- Data/IT Analyst – lineage and data dictionary to ensure summary to detail clarity

This list highlights only some audience requirements and many more could exist in your enterprise. Also, it is worth noting that a person can be in many personas, especially as the data topic changes. For example, a finance analyst might have deep skills in their finance domain. However, for overall company sales performance, the same analyst may be a casual consumer and require more context to understand anything in the sales domain. The domain and context will often determine how you treat your audience.

Figure 2.3: The Three Is of Visualization Value – audience effort and steps

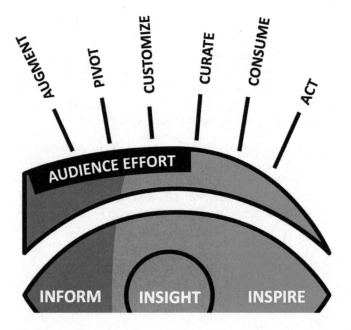

Audience Effort

The audience also has stages they follow depending on how much the analyst has provided them. The success of the audience relies on their skills and ability to leverage the software and data that they have access to, as seen in Figure 2.3. The following are the steps the audience often take in their data journey:

1. Augment – most data may be pre-processed; however, an additional spreadsheet may be needed to answer their question. They require ability to add data and merge perspectives to create the required views.
2. Pivot – all data may be loaded and transformed already; however, some calculations and summarization may be required to support their needs.
3. Customize – perform simple interactions with existing data visualization; however, additional personalization with filters and preferred graphs and displays may occur.
4. Curate – save a copy of the original data visualization and add context or provide overlay of insight to enhance understanding. Pulling apart complex data visualizations to select the best fit for usage.

5. Consume – simply rely on the data visualization provided as this is close to what is required. However, this may require accessing more than one data visualization to get all needs met.

6. Act – inspired to take required action from the data visualization to drive decisions at the speed of thought.

Completing the Model

This book uses the **Three Is** model throughout as a consistent reference point when stepping through software features and worked examples. Each *Visualization Value level* will be identified for the analyst and the audience through the book. Samples are provided to reuse, and all the examples aim to assist you in building your skills by practicing some of the tips and approaches. There are some drag-and-drop examples, some extensions using code and APIs, and some data wrangling of open data sources. There is something for all SAS users, no matter your skill level and experience as you progress on your skills journey throughout the book.

You can now see that a variety of skills are required depending on the type of value delivered from the data visualization. As seen in Figure 2.4, all the effort and steps can be mapped for each persona to show the skills involved in getting the desired value. Ultimately, the more skills each persona has, the less reliant they are on the other. Also, if the data visualization is designed with this value scale in mind, the audience has the least effort required to proceed on their data journey.

Figure 2.4: The Three Is of Visualization Value – completed model

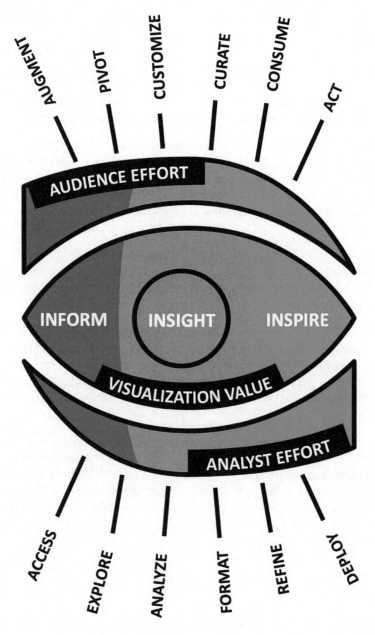

Importance of Skills Development

Over recent years, there has been a movement back toward coding being a superpower, which is excellent for the engagement of youth in STEM pursuits. However, we need to realize that the workforce has, and will continue to have, smart people who are not coders. These people, with the right support of software tools, can develop excellent literacy in the outcomes of AI and analytics without the need to head back to school to become a developer. Also, we cannot afford to start every data to decision process with a line of code – we need to jump to the decision part of the analysis and that is the power of a well-designed data visualization.

The use of data visualization is continuing to grow because organizations have not arrived at their desired data journey destination yet. Organizations continue to pour money into data and storage without focusing in on the core requirement: *answers*. The data journey has a continued focus from SAS, and our goal is to allow your organization to get all of the workforce engaged with data and provide a set of software tools that allow any persona to grow their skills into all areas of data literacy.

The question arises, where do you fit in this role definition? The short answer is: "it depends." You may find your skills are great as an analyst in your domain and field; however, to learn more about other fields and data sets, you are the audience. This means we all need to be mindful of where we are in assessing the dashboard or data visualization that we are looking at.

There is a well-documented skills gap in the data science market and the disruption to many industries is already seeing displacement across traditional jobs and markets (Lazio and Ford 2019). This skills gap is an important focus, and many programs and countries are pivoting to adjust for this. Clearly, we need to move faster, and software can assist with this skills readiness, but smarter software is the key. Not everyone is a coder. However, we need AI-literate non-coders in the world.

Do not despair if you are the person who feels their data skills could be developed further. There has been an explosion in skills and courses focused on data and AI. Business Analytics is now a common program in colleges and universities across the globe. SAS partners with many academic institutions globally to provide access to course content and software to continue this skills pathway (Radu 2018). SAS also created certifications for business users and programmers using the latest SAS tools and techniques.

Rise of AI and the Role of Automation and Skills Augmentation

In a skills context, the rise of AI to suggest data analysis actions and prompt the user for a decision is great, and SAS continues to invest in these AI assistants throughout the software. AI is currently allowing accelerated skills development from data, exploration, format, and design of the information. It is not magic, however, and the quality of the decisions from the human analyst is still the key to inspire the audience.

As AI is embedded more and more across all parts of software, you can expect that the skills required by the users of the software would be lessened. This journey is early, and as we all know based on recommendations in our online shopping sites – there is room for improvement before the human creativity and context is replaced.

The new international language is data. Data and how to leverage data are the new literacy requirements. Knowing how to ask the right questions of the available data is important, and knowing why the insights matter is equally important. This, like any discipline, takes practice and training and skills improve over time.

Conclusion

Thinking of the data journey from the perspective of the analyst and the audience allows all users to see things from their own familiar lens and hopefully allowing them to see things from an alternate lens. The Three-I model is meant to assist us in understanding the value that we get from data visualizations and the effort that it takes to get the value. If we go into data projects with this in mind from the beginning, the value and impact from your visualizations will improve. Remember, reading this book is investing in your skills development as you move along your own journey with SAS.

References

"Infographic: The Data Scientist Shortage." 2018. insideBIGDATA, August 19, 2018.
    https://insidebigdata.com/2018/08/19/infographic-data-scientist-shortage/

Isaacson, Walter. 2014. *The Innovators: How a Group of Hackers, Geniuses, and Geeks Created the Digital Revolution.*
    New York: Simon & Schuster.

Lazio, Rick and Ford, Harold Jr. 2019. "The Economic Imperative of Reforming STEM Education." Scientific American.
    October 1, 2019. https://www.scientificamerican.com/article/the-economic-imperative-of-reforming-stem-
    education/

Radu, Alex. 2018. "SAS CEO Jim Goodnight on the importance of education, STEM, and ending the skills gap." IT World
    Canada, March 29, 2018. https://www.itworldcanada.com/article/sas-ceo-jim-goodnight-on-the-importance-of-
    education-stem-and-ending-the-skills-gap/402248

Chapter 3: SAS and Data Visualization

Overview

The purpose of this chapter is to provide an overview of SAS and its history providing intelligent dashboards, reports, and visualization for businesses across the globe. We will discuss some of SAS products and what they included to achieve dashboards and reports. This chapter will illustrate that SAS has been creating software for generations of analysts to analyze and share insights through data visualization.

Audience

This chapter provides for the novice or advanced SAS user a historical context and timely reference of what can be achieved by reading this book with SAS.

> *"Most of us need to listen to the music to understand how beautiful it is. But often that's how we present statistics: we just show the notes, we don't play the music."*

Hans Rosling

Introduction

Famous TED talk presenter Hans Rosling inspired many with his evangelism of designing data visualization with clarity and engaging story telling with health statistics. Many of you might also know that SAS has a rich history with dashboards and data visualization capabilities that have often been overshadowed with expertise in machine learning (ML) and statistical analysis. Early on, SAS recognized that sharing the insights generated from data analysis was critical and also that data visualization was important to analysts and end users. This chapter talks through the present capabilities and provides a nod to the past capabilities of SAS in the data visualization arena.

A Short History

SAS and data visualization – some people might say it is a love story for the ages, or others might just say that SAS has been doing dashboards and data visualization for ages. Since SAS was incorporated in 1976, a core principal has been to apply statistical analysis on data to gain insights. The need for data visualization and graphs was seen early in this journey, which was embodied with the release of SAS/GRAPH in 1980. SAS/GRAPH went on to lead the way for SAS and drive the need for further products to share insights through visualization (WRAL 2011).

Because legacy dashboard capability is the theme of this section, we will focus offerings from SAS that best match this description. The journey from SAS/GRAPH to SAS Visual Analytics was varied and had some notable highlights along this path. The three solutions we believe match the dashboard brief most closely are SAS/GRAPH, SAS Business Intelligence (BI), and SAS Visual Analytics.

SAS/GRAPH

Initially released 1980, this toolset is, to this day, one of the most powerful graphing solutions in the world. Many times, when approaching a data challenge and searching for options, SAS/GRAPH has delivered where many other approaches had not. Many of these capabilities are now embedded into SAS Viya with SAS ODS Graphics Editor and include Graph Template Language (GTL) to create almost limitless outputs and combinations.

Figure 3.1: Sample sales dashboard – SAS/GRAPH (SAS 2020)

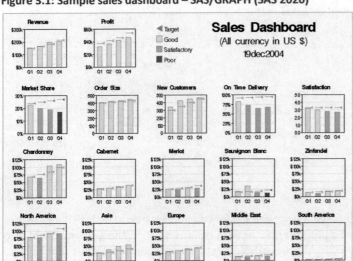

SAS Business Intelligence

SAS Web Report Studio – initially released in March 2005, this software was created and leveraged during the first wave of business intelligence, and provided self-service, web browser-based reporting for business. This toolset was delivered as part of a suite of data, analytics, and administration solutions from SAS and sold as part of the SAS BI Server and SAS Enterprise BI Server bundles. SAS Web Report Viewer was available to SAS customers who only licensed the SAS Information Delivery Portal and not SAS Web Report Studio. This offering was great because you could aggregate content from OLAP cubes, SAS data sets, or directly from data source. This included powerful formatting to build dashboard-like interactive reports.

Figure 3.2: SAS Web Report Studio – sample report example (Aanderud and Hall 2011)

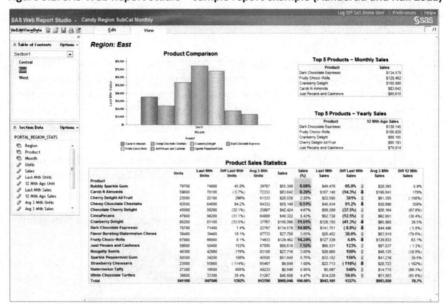

SAS Information Delivery Portal – Like other portal technology, the SAS portal was a content aggregator and content delivery system. This provided a dashboard look and feel to SAS and non-SAS content all in one end-user experience. For example, you could combine a coded graph task next to a SAS Web Report Studio report with an HTML web page, all presented to the user as a dashboard. This was such a functional and central toolset for all the SAS ecosystem and allowed some amazing extensions to be developed and shared for all customers to use. Similar to a software development kit (SDK), customers could innovate with powerful portlet extensions. In fact, one of the first collaborations for the authors of this book was creating a functional portlet to use in the SAS Information Delivery Portal. We worked together to create the Stored Process Editor Portlet extension for a better end-user experience as seen in Figure 3.3. This portlet allowed the SAS code to be edited by approved users right there, where the content was displayed inside the portal. The Information Delivery Portal allowed for this innovation using portlet technology and pioneered the dashboard interface.

Figure 3.3: SAS Information Delivery Portal – showing sample data using SAS code via a SAS Stored Process and providing a user interface using a custom portlet (Schulz and Murphy 2009)

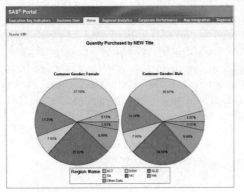

SAS BI Dashboard – Initially released in 2012. Clearly as the need grew to provide a more specific dashboard experience and introduce animation into the audience experience, SAS released a companion toolset called SAS BI Dashboard. To achieve this, the toolset was initially developed using Adobe Flash/Flex, which was a relevant technology at that time. This addition to the SAS solutions made a great companion for the other offerings in the business intelligence age and provided the audience with a "wow" factor with dancing gauges and graphs. Once again, this tool acted as an aggregation layer for the other SAS analytics platform solutions. A bit of further trivia to note is this toolset was developed by Falko Schulz, who is one of this book's authors. Falko is currently a developer on the SAS Visual Analytics products.

Figure 3.4: SAS BI Dashboard – Creating a summary collection of data visualization in a dashboard format has been part of SAS for decades

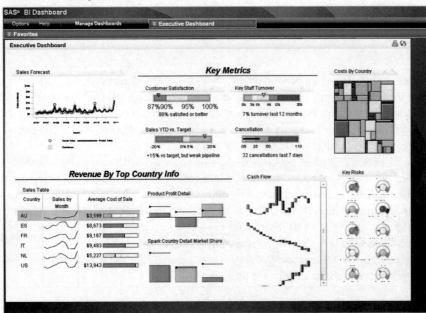

SAS has embedded data visualization capabilities into almost all offerings since then, including solutions in machine learning, data discovery, data management, administration, real-time engines, risk solutions, fraud and security solutions, and so much more! Creating a dashboard with SAS is not a new idea, and creating a collection of graphics and tables to tell a comprehensive and interconnected view of a business problem has been a core use of SAS software for decades. SAS was founded on the goals of applying math and statistics to business challenges. SAS realized early that communicating these insights to the stakeholders across a business was important to taking action based on facts.

For more than 40 years, SAS has been creating dashboards, reports, and data visualizations providing users of all skills the right software for each challenge. SAS loves dashboards, and this quick walk through history helps you understand how SAS has powered data visualization. This chapter is not aiming to provide a distinct list of tools from SAS and the dates of their releases, but rather, the intent here is to show the many ways SAS evolved in capability over the history of the company and how dashboard style visualizations have played a core part of this journey.

SAS Visual Analytics

A core solution for dashboards and data visualization from SAS is SAS Visual Analytics, which provides a single application for data exploration, analysis, and reporting. SAS Visual Analytics is powered by SAS Viya and provides almost endless ways to explore and visualize data. This book focuses on using SAS Visual Analytics to create an impactful data journey for your audience. With SAS Visual Analytics, you can streamline both the discovery and creation process for the analyst, while providing many options for your audience to be able to consume and understand the information being shared.

SAS Visual Analytics provides many benefits including these key capabilities:

- **Reports and dashboards** – You can design reports once and distribute and publish them anywhere – web, mobile, API, or even Microsoft Office.

- **Interactive charts and visualization** – You can deliver insights from any size and type of data in a simple visual element from bar charts, geographic maps, or even a single highlighted number.

- **Visual data preparation and transformation** – You can import data from anywhere and transform the data to match your needs without leaving your report.

- **Powerful, easy-to-use analytics** – Many embedded self-service artificial intelligence (AI) and machine learning (ML) functions are available to enhance the traditional business analysis, including forecasting, text analytics, network analysis, and much more.

- **Open and extensible** – New application programming interface (API) options enable you to embed external visualizations and embed SAS Visual Analytics into any application not from SAS, which provides almost endless entry and exit points for your projects. You can get inspired from API examples provided on SAS website.

- **Custom visuals** – More out-of-the-box visuals than ever before are provided, including a built-in graph builder and custom visuals that use third-party data-driven content. These visuals will bring your data journey to life for your audience.

- **Advanced location analytics** – SAS Visual Analytics leverages GIS mapping technologies provided by Esri to provide visualization and data enrichment using geospatial objects.

SAS Visual Analytics provides a single solution for many use cases, and it also allows analysts to grow their skills and their understanding of analytics without leaving a consistent and visual user interface. There are many more capabilities included in SAS Visual Analytics. This book focuses on using SAS Visual Analytics and provides many examples to demonstrate these capabilities.

Before we look past SAS Visual Analytics, it is worth a quick reflection on the road traveled. In its current release, SAS Visual Analytics provides embedded AI and BI elements for audience and analysts across the globe and is a leading solution what unlocks many of the SAS Viya capabilities. This was not achieved overnight and has been a journey with some amazing contributions from SAS developers and driven by SAS customer's requirements over many years. See Figure 3.5 to see the release history of SAS Visual Analytics.

Figure 3.5: SAS Visual Analytics release history (SAS 2020)

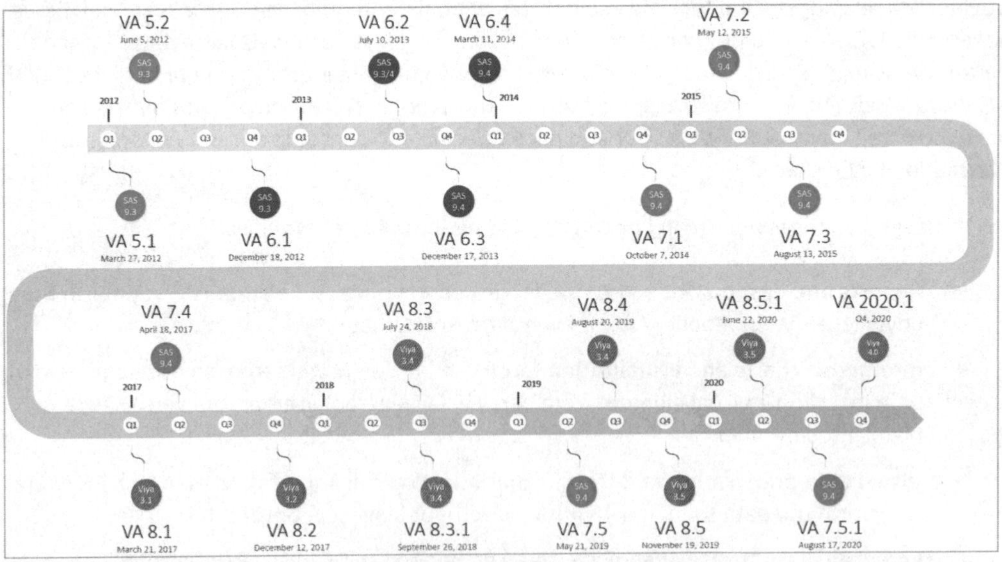

It is worth noting that SAS R&D is changing the way it approaches product and code development. You can see in Figure 3.5 that the version numbers have changed with this new approach. With the success of DevOps, which describes the Development Operations for software development, starting with SAS Viya 4, R&D applies the concept of Continuous Integration/Continuous Delivery. This means developers will update the underlying product code every day, test it, and re-deploy. Once done, the process starts all over again – every day, every week, and month. While SAS is not releasing a new product version every day, the cycle of product updates will be much shorter than in the past, giving customers access to new features and potential bug fixes much quicker. In order to support such continuous delivery, a number of automated processes have been implemented to support auto deployment, test and validation.

> **TIP: SAS Enterprise Guide**
>
> There are other software solutions from SAS which we have omitted in this chapter that could also be included. One favorite is SAS Enterprise Guide, which is a popular part of the SAS suite and contains so many powerful features for analysis and visualization that it needs to be mentioned here. SAS Enterprise Guide has some powerful features that enable access to software like SAS/GRAPH and overlay some additional features to format and assemble data visualizations and reports for the business user. Automation and process flows can simplify creation and sharing of analysis and visualization tasks. Capabilities are designed for both the business user and the programmer alike with wizards and code generation included. It is one of our favorite SAS solutions, and experts from across SAS have published dedicated timelines that provide a very detailed history of SAS Enterprise Guide releases. One of our favorites is found on Chris Hemedinger's blog: *The SAS Dummy* (Hemedinger 2013).

Conclusion

This chapter highlights SAS's commitment to data visualization and exploration. SAS is a business analytics toolset always focused on the business teams and communicating the insight from the complex computations under the hood. The remainder of the book focuses on the current state of data visualization capabilities in the SAS Viya era; however, it is important to recognize the past solutions also. The continued commitment over time from SAS to providing the analysts and their audience with the best experiences over many years. Impactful data journeys require broad capabilities across data, discovery and deployment. Next, we examine the importance of a modern analytics platform that involves more than a dashboard.

References

Aanderud, Tricia and Angela Hall. 2012. *Building Business Intelligence Using SAS®: Content Development Examples*. SAS Institute Inc., Cary, North Carolina, USA.

Hemedinger, Chris. 2013. "Through the years: SAS Enterprise Guide versions", The SAS Dummy, August 6 2013, https://blogs.sas.com/content/sasdummy/2013/08/06/eg-versions-through-years

Rosling, Hans. 2007. "Turning Statistics into Knowledge." Paper presented at the Second OECD World Forum on "Statistics, Knowledge and Policy." June 2007. Istanbul, Turkey.

SAS. n.d. "SAS/GRAPH Dashboard Samples", SAS.com, Accessed 20 April 2020, http://support.sas.com/rnd/datavisualization/dashboards/

SAS. n.d. "SAS® Visual Analytics 8.5: Reference", SAS.com, Accessed 30 April 2020, https://documentation.sas.com/?docsetId=varef&docsetTarget=p0jw6yvvmgogtwn1dnisuidw0jcp.htm&docsetVersion=8.5&locale=en

Schulz, Falko and Travis Murphy. 2009. "Stored Process Editor Portlet." Custom developed portlet, https://go.documentation.sas.com/?docsetId=biwaag&docsetTarget=ag_portlet_table.htm&docsetVersion=9.4&locale=en

WRAL.com. 2011. "SAS Corporate Timeline." March 3, 2011. https://www.wral.com/business/story/9211429/

Chapter 4: The Analytics Life Cycle with SAS Viya

Overview

This chapter highlights the value of a comprehensive analytics ecosystem and how data visualization fits into this. You will see the capabilities of SAS Viya and how they all fit together, while maintaining a focus on the dashboard's capability for analyst and audience. This chapter steps through an overview of general capabilities of SAS Viya not just for dashboards, but rather within the entire analytics ecosystem.

Audience

We provide additional ideas of capability within SAS Viya for different user requirements to solve the broad challenges for data journeys, which is applicable to all SAS users.

> *"If analytics is the engine of change, data is the fuel ... the opportunity is enormous."*
>
> *Jim Goodnight*

Introduction

The power of visualization to support decisions where they are made is important. It is equally important to understand that visualization is not enough on its own and needs a complete set of capabilities to support your analytics culture. As the quote from Dr. Goodnight illustrates, data without analytics is nothing more than a raw material. The combination of data and analytics together are where value is realized. Your analytics platform ensures that the value is realized over and over again. A modern enterprise needs to have a robust analytics platform to ensure they can meet both the demands of today and the ever-changing requirements of tomorrow. SAS provides powerful analytical capabilities for end users across the enterprise, from data scientists to business analysts to information consumers.

Having all users participate in the same platform has many benefits, and it allows development of skills across the enterprise as people change roles or as they continue to require analytics to support their decisions. Your analytics platform needs to provide your users and audience with choices while keeping your enterprise under control at the same time. Choice and control are both important benefits of SAS Viya. All roles are covered for the analytics life cycle through data, discovery, deployment, and orchestration. An analytics platform covers all stages of the analytics life cycle. We will step through these components in more detail.

Choice and Control

That perfect balance of choice and control is what gives organizations the ability to accelerate the analytics life cycle. Organizations need a platform that fully supports all phases of data, discovery, and deployment regardless of what data is being used, the analytics being leveraged, or how the models are being deployed. This is what the SAS platform does. A comprehensive analytics platform can help ask the right questions, find the right answers, and get tangible results from analytics.

It might help to think about a platform addressing the following:

- The ever-changing analytic ecosystem.
- The volume, variety, and velocity of data.
- IT and Business teams trying to deploy and sustain the required analytical models.

In an analytics context, it becomes very clear that when you have too much choice then effective progress is impaired for an enterprise. It continues to be true that if controls are too tight then innovation can come to a standstill. It is important that your analytics platform provides choice and control in the right measure to reach the potential with data-driven processes. We will step through why your data journeys require more than just a dashboard tool by offering choice and control for all steps along this path.

Choice

Organizations need to have the freedom to choose languages, tools, data, techniques, and environments because this is what drives innovation and creativity.   This provides an open workspace to innovate, to tackle new challenges, to explore the data and see what answers it contains. A wide range of employees need to be able to take advantage of all these choices, regardless of their analytic skill set.

Choice is important to allow all employees to participate in your analytics culture. Recruitment of new staff and retaining existing staff are a challenge in STEM fields, so by having an open analytics ecosystem, you can focus on the talent and not the tools. Analytic culture needs to be inclusive and welcome everyone, no matter their previous experience.

Elements of choice include:

- Programming languages – use languages across the analytics ecosystem in one place like Python, R, SAS, and more
- Talent and skills – leverage analytics skills broader than specific software
- Code or User Interface – allow users to choose how they solve data challenges
- Analytic techniques – analytics is a continuum that requires a strong framework
- Data sources – data type, structure, and source are everywhere and change regularly

Control

We do not see choice and control as opposing platform qualities as they are inter-connected. What is critical is that there is a balance of choice and control for your organization in order to execute your analytic strategy and drive real world results. However, if there are no controls in place, many issues can quickly overcome an organization.

Controls are necessary to provide trust in the data and analytical processes, which once lost, is very hard to get the trust back. Businesses must trust that results of models are accurate and that the models will continue to perform over time. As a result, transparency, governance, and security are essential. Controls become even more critical as organizations attempt to drive digital transformation processes with analytics.

Controls consist of elements like:

- Data and model governance – quality of models and accuracy over time is critical
- Deployment capabilities – Apps, APIs, interactive user interfaces, and data visualization options without changing underlying models
- Security and privacy – compliance with privacy regulations like GDPR require enterprise-grade security
- Scalability – big data is everywhere, and the analytic platform needs to perform no matter the situation

Accelerate the Analytics Life Cycle

SAS may have started as a coded language for data analysis; however, the modern SAS is open and covers many analytic and data users and skills, all with a common goal for secured and governed access and use of data and the resultant impact that data has. Let us step through the components of the analytics life cycle to better understand the steps and stages of a data journey that need to be considered. The analytics life cycle can best be thought of in the following steps of data, discovery, deployment, and orchestration as seen in Figure 4.1.

Figure 4.1: Accelerate the analytics life cycle with SAS Viya

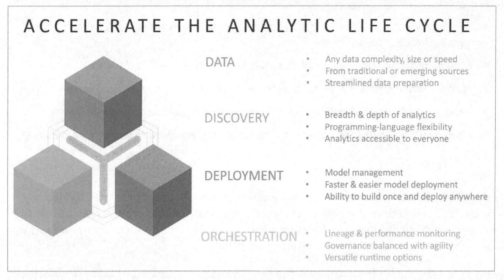

We will quickly step through these components of the analytics life cycle.

Data: Fuel for Decisions

Data holds so much opportunity for organizations to solve many problems and support digital transformation. This requires the organization to enable access to all available and relevant data. SAS Viya helps deliver cleansed, governed, real-time data from all your sources. This enables your analytics to perform across the entire organization.

Discovery: Revving the Engine

Analysis is what enriches your data and gives context. You want a broad analytics toolbox with a deep and wide set of proven analytics capabilities for a wide variety of users. SAS provides a wide set of analytical capabilities: from statistics to machine learning (ML) and from cognitive programming in SAS to open-source languages for analytics.

Deployment: Build Once, Use Everywhere

Data and insight are worth very little if your organization cannot make it a core part of business operations. SAS empowers you to integrate analytical results and insights back into your organization with speed and at scale, from the simple to the most complex operating environments.

Orchestration: Ensuring Trusted Decisions

Orchestration requires pulling all elements of the analytics life cycle together and is often the most underrated element of an analytics platform. Orchestration encompasses data lineage, model performance monitoring, robust governance regardless of the analytical language or data source, and this includes executing the analytical processes as close to the data as required without transfer of duplication. This operationalization process for analytics is so important to achieve digital transformation. SAS Viya connects and accelerates the activities of the analytics life cycle by providing a broad range of capabilities in one platform.

All these components are important and have many subcomponents to power the enterprise. Figure 4.2 shows some of these subcomponents and where they fit into the platform. As you can see, there are many facets in the data journey which the platform provides.

Figure 4.2: Orchestrate your entire analytics journey – SAS Viya provides a complete analytics and AI enterprise platform

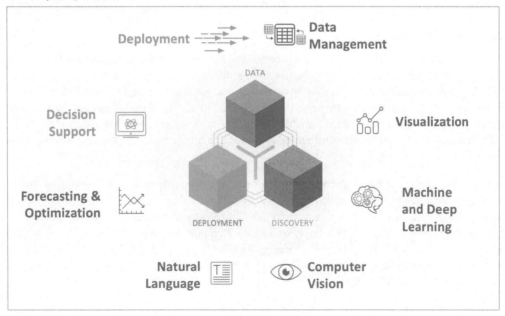

Powering Digital Transformation

Recent history has shown that improvements in AI and ML are at the heart of innovation across the globe. Big data and analytics provide the key to advancement of humankind and is showing business and government a clear pathway to digital transformation. Digital transformation requires some key strategies across the enterprise:

- People – Focusing on skills and talent retention is important and setting up the correct structures and teams to foster autonomy and innovation.
- Strategy – Your go-to-market approach needs to ensure that data is at the heart of interactions. How your internal processes support your enhanced digital customer experience is essential.
- Technology – Ensuring your core systems are modern and can leverage your analytics engine to support and innovate your customer interactions.

No matter your current state of digital transformation, SAS can power many critical decisions and processes. Across areas like fraud and security intelligence, risk management, customer intelligence, retail, Data for Good, health care, Internet of Things, and more across many industries (SAS n.d.). SAS Viya powers these industry and core business solutions including SAS Visual Analytics. It is a privilege to work with customers to solve critical challenges that face the modern world using data and analytics.

Conclusion

As mentioned, visual interfaces form a great benefit of the SAS platform and pull capabilities across the entire platform for growing the use of AI and analytics throughout the enterprise. This book is focused primarily on the SAS Visual Analytics, and we also leverage some API and web services through code as we step through the examples. The ability to communicate data to your audience is critical to support digital transformation. We look at functionality included to assist the analyst and the audience with embedded AI and ML to bridge the skills gap and leap to faster insights from data.

This chapter outlined the benefits and capabilities within an enterprise analytics platform. The analyst and the audience are provided room to grow and flourish with a consistent and secure suite of software to allow for innovation and a skills journey to take place. Whilst dashboards and data visualization are a key element of any analytics platform, we need to see the benefits of these capabilities within a broader critical engine for the enterprise. Analytical skills are a huge part of enterprise success in the new world of AI whilst still allowing the business to conduct a traditional business intelligence journey.

References

Greiner, Lynn. 2017. "'The engine of change': SAS Institute says it wants to bring its analytics everywhere." Financial Post, Apr 17, 2017. https://financialpost.com/technology/cio/the-engine-of-change-sas-institute-says-it-wants-to-bring-its-analytics-everywhere

SAS. n.d. "SAS Viya & the Analytics Life Cycle." Accessed 20 April 2020. https://www.sas.com/en_us/software/platform/analytics-life-cycle.html

SAS. n.d. "DATA FOR GOOD: Analytics helping humanity." Accessed August 2, 2020. https://www.sas.com/en_us/data-for-good.html.

Chapter 5: Design Approaches

Overview

The aim of this chapter is to outline the importance of design and the ability to strike a balance between a robust and repeatable data-driven approach when designing a data visualization. This chapter explores the value of telling a story to match your audience, and not at the expense of your message. We look at how graphic design sensibilities are useful in business today when they do not take away from the clarity of the message being shared from the data.

Audience

This chapter is designed for all SAS skill levels. This provides an important foundation for the remainder of the book and your journey in creating data visualization with SAS Viya.

> *"Clutter and confusion are failures of design, not attributes of information."*

> *Edward Tufte*

Introduction

The problem today is that information is everywhere, so it is no longer just about serving up an accurate number. The story that wraps that number in context is more important than ever. While we have many ways to tell this story, most require you to verbally or textually explain the story. This is the most common option today and is why we are inundated with email and social media as we struggle to understand what is being served up in written form. The other way to tell stories is using visualizations, which are often done poorly, as we all have seen in a presentation slide that contains a thousand words on a single screen. The challenge of today is to combine language and visualization to tell impactful stories that the audience responds to. We have seen a rise in social media tiles and infographics to help cut through the noise and get to the point. These infographics leverage data, language, and visualization to create just enough content to tell the story in the shortest possible way.

Infographics have been used for a long time; however, in today's world, the information and channels are so crowded that you can no longer rely on the glue of language to make up for poor data visualization. The human being will fill in any gaps in the story with assumptions or confusion, as is our nature. As the analyst, you are now required to ensure your data visualizations hit the mark every time with the audience. The real question is how to ensure you are hitting the mark with your data visualization creations.

As the quote from Tufte at the start of this chapter explains, you should be clear in how you represent the data in your data visualization projects, and do not introduce clutter or confusion with your design decisions.

Choosing the Right Data Output

This book is about data visualization. However, there are many data options for the audience, and choosing the *right* output can be a challenge. Not all data projects require customized outputs from analysts. However, they all require clarity. Clarity in the message and key insights is key to the audience noticing and actioning what you are trying to tell them. Lack of clarity is often what leads to information missing your audience and becoming a "so what" reaction.

Consider the types of information products that often contain data, and think about how these work in your enterprise to tell the story of that data. Everything does not have to be a data visualization and may be solved with less effort and time. You could think about the following alternatives for your audience:

- **Email** – Email is often the executive's main source of information. Often, an alert or a single data point can be consumed and actioned quickly.

- **Presentation** – Business teams use presentations today to combine data and narrative to tell a story and share this with stakeholders. An embedded number or table can be fast and actionable.

- **Infographic** – Infographics are an output that has gained popularity in the business world in recent years and are proven to have impact with data.

- **Report or dashboard** –Reports like monthly sales have been widely used in the business intelligence world to provide answers to common questions.

- **Formatted spreadsheet** – The spreadsheet is great for personal productivity and is relied upon for many data decisions in businesses across the globe.

- **Unformatted spreadsheet** – You could call this a "data dump," but it might be exactly what a savvy audience needs to get to the heart of the question.

- **Application features** – Many modern software tools have powerful data included within the application itself and might be enough to answer the questions.

- **Data source access** – Depending on the data, access source data or connect to a data extract to push to another system.

In summary, the audience has options in how they receive their information and special requirements depending on their own preferences. For example, some people love podcasts, and some love reading newspapers, which does not mean that either is wrong, just different. We all have preferences to how we get our information. Our audience demands are changing as the information world around them also changes, and we need to adapt how we approach data projects.

Humans Are Visual Creatures

Humans are visual creatures, but this does not mean that every analyst needs to be a graphic artist. The tools today need to be able to ensure options and shortcuts for data teams to produce these impactful and appealing data visualizations for their audience. It does mean that we need to modernize our approach to the data projects that we produce and be mindful of the visual and user experience that we create for our audience. We can all learn from the rise in data-driven infographics and journalism around us today because this has raised the bar of audience expectations, and we need to rise to meet those expectations.

There are many times someone says that they are a visual learner or that they have read the theory that people understand visual communication better than any other format. In research for this book, we came across many perspectives that share this basic point of view. This is one of the reasons humans need supporting data visualization to help with our understanding of complex topics and data challenges. Our research shows us that half the human brain is involved with visual processing and that 70% of all sensory receptors are located in the eyes (Merieb and Hoehn 2007). If humans are relying so much on visual processing and we only have about one-tenth of a second before the audience has processed a visual scenario, then we should be inspired to make the initial view of a data visualization the most visually appealing to increase the chance of being impactful to the audience (Semetko and Scammell 2012).

While we are all informavores, we are not all designers. However, there are some great design ideas that we can use to ensure what we create increases our chances of more impact. Creating beautiful reports and dashboards is a way to address this for data analysts and a few things to consider are outlined in the following section (SAS 2020).

Tips for Insightful Data Visualization

Designing compelling dashboards and reports is situational and requires you to know your audience. This is not different than any storytelling where you need to know who the target audience is to resonate. However, there are some elements that are used in a data visualization which we will highlight here and use later in the book with worked examples.

- **Be creative** – don't be boxed in with your first step. That might happen later down the path, but initially think like a child and create without restriction.

- **Build a facts hierarchy** – present a main fact first, then reveal the less important facts.

- **Add visual elements** – combine data driven elements and non-data elements.

- **Showcase what's important** – use large and small objects to assist the audience.

- **Edit your work** – don't be afraid to remove objects after you have started. What you choose to omit might be the best decision that you make.

- **Color matters** – use color to highlight the relevant facts or data. Don't go color crazy or you risk distracting the audience from your intended information. A general rule is to stick to a defined color palette with generally no more than 3-5 colors. Search for "online palette builders" to find resources to help you design your own color schemes.

- **Add context** – thinking about the way data is processed by humans, you must provide instant context for the audience. Consider adding descriptions and labels to assist navigation.

- **Be consistent** – your audience will learn the style of your storytelling – you don't need to be revolutionary every time in business communications.

- **Learn from your users** – what are audiences tuning into at your organization? Run an administrator's report on the most popular reports then segment audience by role level or type to see what is rating (a television term). This means you will have market intelligence on what users want and where they consume.

- **Seek Feedback** – a designer will take time to create ideas before working through the brief Designers show ideas to their customers to narrow the direction before putting all the effort in. Data visualization is no different as you can quickly get some examples of styles or layouts that might narrow how the audience expects to navigate this data journey – before you waste hours in getting something they don't even want prepared.

- **Be accurate** – one of the biggest issues with business information is trust – your brand inside your organization will be made or broken on the accuracy of the facts that you are presenting. That said, we can only use the data that we have at that time, and you can always keep improving the quality and processes whilst your team looks to add new sources or better data marts.

- **Have a vision** – you might not be the best at all parts of this project, but be true to the vision and rely on the other experts in your team to help you achieve it.

- **Communicate** – the thing that kills many projects is a lack of communication.

- **Be agile** – iterate and keep things moving.

One way to increase your skills is to be open to new inputs. You might never have been interested in design, art, or architecture, but being open to new inputs is a great way to improve your own design skills that will make your dashboards and reports a little better. Also invest in your own skills with the technology because the more you know about how to achieve the design that you want, the faster you will be at both the design process and the build process. Knowledge of the software stops you from overcommitting early in the design process, and this same knowledge allows you to over deliver in the final data visualization. The world is changing at a fierce pace, and taking some of these steps will help you build on your own strengths today and take your skills to the next level for tomorrow. Each data visualization you create needs to be fit for purpose. You have different use cases for data visualizations, and this means that there are different elements that should be considered.

Learn from Other Approaches

It is important to look at other disciplines when you are trying to improve your own core skills. Think of this like cross training in sports. In data visualization, we leverage many similar concepts from other artistic and scientific design professions. We could step through many of approaches used in other professions; however, we decided to add three important approaches in this section: rule of thirds, golden ratio, and force-directed algorithm. We will spend some time to see these in action.

Art and Photography Approach

The rule of thirds is a photography approach to framing the perfect shots. The concept essentially creates and 3x3 grid over your design to ensure you balance the elements in the available canvas. The rule of thirds provides a useful start for creating impressive layouts for your data projects. Figure 5.1 shows an example of the rule of thirds used in photography. (Gendelman 2015)

Figure 5.1: Photography and the rule of thirds – overlay on a photograph clearly shows the balance of great photography

This photographer's approach provides some simple guidance for designing your next data visualization. Figure 5.2 shows a data visualization example that illustrates how you can use this technique to check your data visualization proportions and layout. If you are in doubt, use the four intersections of the lines as a starting guide. If your data visualization is more complex, then you can start to move elements into each square.

Figure 5.2: Rule of thirds with a data visualization – applying a 3x3 is a great check for your data visualization design early in the project

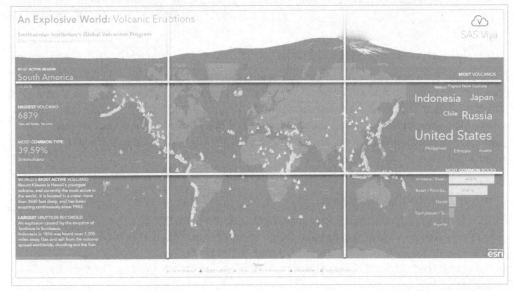

Using this grid approach is flexible yet structured as shown in Figure 5.3. The rule of thirds grid can be used by leveraging the white space (the boxes themselves) or the intersections of the grid. You could place your graphs in one or more boxes and if this does not look balanced and appealing, then look at placing the objects over the intersections of the grid lines. Many data visualization designs use a hybrid approach of the grid elements, which is often trial and error to get the balanced results.

Figure 5.3: Data visualization example layouts with rule of thirds approach

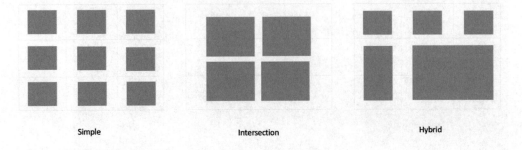

Simple   Intersection   Hybrid

The rule of thirds is only a guide and you will follow your own intuition as long as you are focused on your audience and their experience. If your visualization still does not look appropriate, maybe the next technique is more applicable.

Universal Patterns Approach

There really is no better combination of data and design than applying the Fibonacci sequence to your data visualization layouts. Before we get to that, you might be aware of the Fibonacci sequence, which is a series of numbers where the next number is the sum of the previous two numbers (so 1, 1, 2, 3, 5, 8, 13, and so on). This sequence has been applied to many problems across the world including computer algorithms for search, data structures, and even graphs. The Fibonacci sequence can be used to explain some complex logarithmic spiral shapes like spiral galaxies, sunflowers, and nautilus shells as seen in Figure 5.4. The results of this sequence are known as the golden ratio.

Figure 5.4: The golden ratio in a spiral similar to the nautilus shell is an example of an approximation of a logarithmic spiral using the Fibonacci sequence

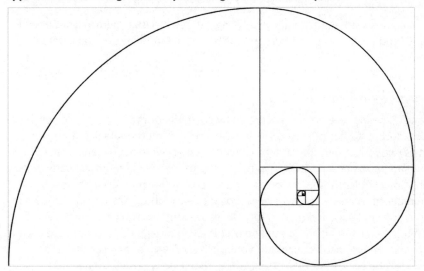

Analysts can also apply the Fibonacci numbers to assist in balance of a design over a data visualization layout. The golden ratio provides an excellent balance to your data visualization designs. It is amazing how naturally this design concepts fits with many data projects that we have produced. The reason this works is because of the golden ratio and as seen in Figure 5.5, the golden rectangle highlights the simplicity of the golden ratio for data visualization designs. The golden ratio will provide your designs with balance and clarity, which your audience will appreciate (Johnson 2010).

Figure 5.5: The golden rectangle clearly maps to the grid-like designs of a data visualization

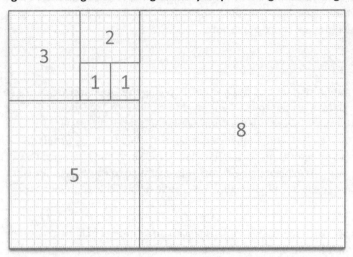

The golden ratio can be followed quite literally by placing a graph or visual element into one of the designated zones, and you can see how this creates balanced interactive or static data visualizations.

Engineering Design Approach

Design principles and guidelines are not always driven by creativity or art. You can also consider established technical design studies or methods and follow related methodologies. Some data visualizations such as network graphs follow such concepts when laying out or rendering data values. In a network plot, nodes are positioned in relation to each other and typically driven by an underlying force-directed algorithm. This means that nodes with higher force, for instance driven by higher number of connections, are placed closer to each other. The example shown in Figure 5.6 represents such network and related force-based layout algorithms. Attention is immediately drawn to central and highly connected nodes. Even though this example uses colors for both nodes and links, you may still notice that you are likely drawn to one specific node in the network. This node labeled "41" represents a central node as it is closely connected to many other nodes. It also represents a so-called "gate-keeper" with it connecting two sub graphs (Wikipedia 2020).

Figure 5.6: Force-directed algorithm applied to a network graph

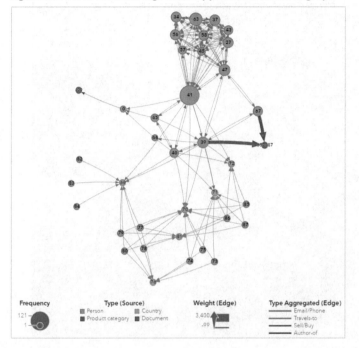

If you keep this principle in mind when designing dashboards or infographics, the business value of each visual element will tell you where to place that item. The underlying concept of force does apply here with higher weighted visualizations in terms of desired impact, placed more dominant or centered. The example infographic shown in Figure 5.7 takes this concept on board with placing the central solar eclipse path visualization in the center of attention.

Figure 5.7: Example infographic with a force-centric design

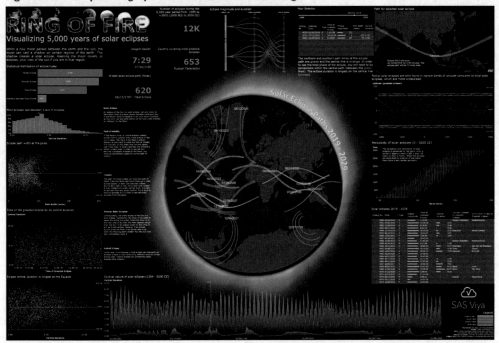

You might also notice that other visualizations are placed around the center main drawing. The idea is that the closer a visualization is to the center, the more important its value is to the business that it represents. However, this does not mean an infographic will always have such centered graphics. The same applies to graphics placed in other parts of the report with the distance to other visualizations describing its value.

This is just a brief look at the rule of thirds, the golden ratio, and force-centric design. We encourage you to research the references in this chapter to learn more. We could include many other design approaches and inspirations from disciplines like user experience, graphic design, and architecture and relate to elements to data visualization projects. These design principles provide analysts a simple way to confirm their dashboards are not trying to do too much in one canvas. The human brain processes the visual scene very quickly. If the initial reaction is not memorable, you might not get another chance to win back that audience again. Taking some time up front to create your design and remove clutter pays off in a huge way when you share your data visualizations.

SAS Visual Analytics Design Tips for Analysts

To achieve many business tasks and build engaging outputs, we rely on software tools. Software tools are synonymous with business and design and have certain behaviors and approaches that make them powerful for these use cases. An example we all leverage each day is a presentation tool like Microsoft PowerPoint. PowerPoint leverages an overlay objects approach, and we use this to impress our audiences in every presentation. For graphic designers, this could be a graphics editing tool like Adobe Photoshop, which also uses layers, amongst other more powerful features, within a project to enable amazing outputs that seem magical to the audience. Similarly, SAS Visual Analytics behaviors unlock certain capabilities and facilitate many of the designs in this book.

To power your SAS Visual Analytics reports, it is worth spending some time to understand general capabilities that assist in achieving your designs. The highlights in this section are not really features, rather they are approaches unlocked by the features of SAS Visual Analytics. To achieve the impactful data visualizations, we leverage some general concepts as follows:

- **Drop zones and containers** – You can achieve a whole lot of formatting by just dragging and dropping in SAS Visual Analytics using intelligent drop zones without the need for containers. You can use the container object in SAS Visual Analytics to group objects together. There are benefits to using both drop zones and container objects. However, when doing precise designs, one or more container objects will provide many options to format and control layout.

- **Object overlay** – A key feature to take advantage of in SAS Visual Analytics when designing infographic data visualizations is the use of object overlay in precision containers. The container object facilitates this concept and the design effect that it allows is impressive. This book covers various examples where the analyst places images over graphs or a graph on another graph. This allows for very creative designs with SAS Visual Analytics and can be the difference between a good data visualization and a great data visualization.

- **Interactivity versus static** – Understanding how your data visualization will be used is going to improve your build process. Typical data visualizations can often be the only tool a user must use to slice and dice data, so interactivity might need to be embedded in the design. If the project is built to provide for a single view of the data, then a static view will suffice. However, SAS Visual Analytics allows flexible interactive navigation for the user if it's enabled using the related options in the Actions pane.

- **One report, many users** – Understanding if you are designing a data visualization for more than one audience can affect the design and might require some additional features to be included. For example, data-driven content objects or parameters assisted navigation allows flexible rendering at run time.

- **New graph options to tell better stories** – SAS Visual Analytics has many out-of-the-box visualizations to use in your design like the key value object, which has an infographic setting to create quick and simple infographic styled elements in your data visualization. You may also leverage many more great visualizations made by others around the globe, given the flexibility the data-driven content object provides.

Specific graphs and objects from SAS Visual Analytics and recommendations of when to use one over another are covered in upcoming chapters. The above set of approaches are included to recommend how to best leverage these graphs and objects in your next data visualization project.

Conclusion

It is clear from our experiences that analysts who look to improve their design skills improve their dashboards and reports. Investing in the tool's features is also a great way to get the desired outcomes in your data project. Impactful data visualizations are not accidental; they are considered from both the audience and the analyst perspective. Increasing your awareness of design principles is a great way to improve your next data visualization project. Next, we start to dissect what should go into your data visualization creations and recommend the elements that you should consider.

References

"Force-directed Graph Drawing." 2020. Wikipedia. Last modified April 14, 2020. https://en.wikipedia.org/wiki/Force-directed_graph_drawing

Byrd, Deborah. 2013. "What's special about the shape of a Nautilus shell?" April 18, 2013. https://earthsky.org/human-world/nautilus-shell-fibonacci-logarithmic-spiral-golden-spiral

Gendelman, Vladimir. 2015. "How to Use the Rule of Thirds Effortlessly", *Company Folders*, July 21, 2015. https://www.companyfolders.com/blog/rule-of-thirds-graphic-design

Johnson, Ross. 2010. "HOW TO DESIGN USING THE FIBONACCI SEQUENCE". 3.7 Designs. October 12, 2010. https://3.7designs.co/blog/2010/10/how-to-design-using-the-fibonacci-sequence/

Marieb, Elaine N., and Katja Hoehn. 2007. *Human Anatomy & Physiology*, 7th ed. San Francisco, CA: Pearson Benjamin Cummings.

SAS. n.d. "Data Can Be Beautiful." Accessed August 1, 2020. https://communities.sas.com/html/assets/breports/index.html.

Semetko, Holli, and Margaret Scammell, editors. 2012. *The SAGE Handbook of Political Communication*. Thousand Oaks, CA: SAGE Publications.

Tufte, Edward. 1990. *Envisioning Information*. Cheshire, CT: Graphics Press.

Chapter 6: Visual Elements

Overview

This chapter explores the elements that make up a data visualization. What we decide to place in a dashboard or data visualization, and often what we decide to omit from a visualization are the core decisions that make a project a success or a failure. The aim of this chapter is to provide some suggestions and insights about what you should place in your next data visualization.

Audience

This chapter will be interesting to both business users and more technical analysts because you will see the approaches of traditional graphs versus analytical driven graphs. You will read about which graphs we recommend for various scenarios and how they can enhance the data journey.

> *"If you're navigating a dense information jungle, coming across a beautiful graphic or a lovely data visualization, it's a relief. It's like coming across a clearing in the jungle."*

David McCandless

Introduction

What makes a great data visualization? Sometimes you just know by looking at a data visualization that it is perfect, and other times you just know that something is off. This can be caused by not following some of the designing data visualization techniques in previous chapter, or it often has to do with the elements included in the data visualization by the analyst. The graph is not the right graph to show the story clearly or there is no context to assist the visuals. These are issues that can be addressed before the audience gets their eyes on the data visualization through careful consideration of what elements go into your design.

As mentioned previously, a great dashboard or data visualization has some simple characteristics. Here are some ideas about what works for users of dashboards and visualization and why they work.

Learn from Infographics

A dashboard is an information application, and like many of the best apps, the best dashboards do not require any additional training or special skills to use. The user can simply open the dashboard or data visualization and start to navigate by clicking and moving on areas that matter or are interesting to the question the audience has. Today, all insight from data is competing for attention, and we only have seconds to provide a reason for the audience to stay. A great data visualization needs to grab the attention of the audience in a similar way that an infographic does. This can be achieved by applying a makeover to existing dashboards or reports and taking some of the characteristics of the infographic and applying these in the build phase of your next visualization project. Elements of your data visualization can be improved by thinking of them as an infographic, and how all the infographic elements pull together on your dashboard to tell a complete and impactful narrative.

Elements of Your Data Visualization

Each data visualization element is crucial in how the audience will interact and understand the data journey that you create for them. These elements can be grouped into two categories: quantitative elements and subjective elements.

Quantitative: Data-Driven Elements

Choosing the right data-driven element is at the heart of an analyst's skill set, and we can all agree we have made some poor choices in previous data projects. There is some art to this selection; however, mostly this is science. The best graph to use for your data is a well-studied field, and you can find entire websites that list charts and which one best represents your data. That said, we still need to be aware of the audience and think about their familiarity and skills to process the visualization to get the impact that you designed for. This category includes charts and graphs, tables, single numbers, and dynamic text. No matter how the data-driven element is used, you should think of the data journey your audience is expected to travel before committing to that element. We spend a large portion of this chapter on explaining quantitative options.

Subjective: Creative Elements

Today with the rise in apps and user experience, analysts continually must improve the look and feel of their data visualization designs. The following are some examples of creative elements that analysts should consider before releasing their data visualization designs to their audience.

- **Icons and Images** – can assist with getting the point across quickly and can act as a reference, analogy, or metaphor. Symbolism and metaphors can be a great way to anchor the message of your data visualizations, and often this means custom icons or images. Text is also a great way to add some context to the data visualization and to provide a layer of understanding. This includes title text and explanatory comments.

- **Branding and Themes** – create an identity for your content. This could also be a way of aligning your themes to the corporate branding of your organization by using the logo or corporate colors. Colors matter for experience, clarity, accessibility, and emotion. Use color to highlight data, rather than to distract the audience. We all struggle with this fine line of color and often use too much color. More color is not always more impact. Ensure that your data visualization is accessible for all users in your organization. Also keep in mind the impact of colors for accessibility. You can find more details about creating accessible reports using SAS Visual Analytics in the user guide (SAS 2020a).

- **User Experience and Object Placement** – is sometimes misplaced or forgotten, but ultimately user experience is what makes the visualization hit its mark. What story are you telling, and how easy is it for the user to see without you being there to guide them? The best infographic dashboards are the ones that work on different levels. Someone who has a quick glance gets something from it, and someone who spends more time gets something extra.

The techniques covered in the designing data visualizations chapter also touch on these subjective techniques; however, these are also elements of your data visualization build and need to be assessed alongside the all other elements.

Deciding Which Visualization to Use

Choosing the right visual object or graph to fit the situation can be hard, yet the path to the right data visualization should be rewarding and simple. This chapter aims to provide some approaches to selecting the right visual for the story you are trying to tell with your data. It is wise to keep the clarity of your message as a guiding principle when choosing the object to best highlight the insight in your data. A graph might not be best for all situations. Instead, you could use an image or a high-level number (key value) to highlight the context of the data. Dynamic text can also be powerful and pull through highlights driven from the data selected. Use a data comprehension test before you build the data visualization – that is, will your audience understand what you are showing in your final design? To help you understand the options that you have available, this chapter will outline some data-driven elements that can be used within SAS to analyze and explore the insight in your data.

A Starting Point

Before we jump into different visuals in SAS, let's pause and think about what your approach is. When starting out with your data, you should really consider the type of data you have and the best way to visualize this data. Are you trying to compare data, show distribution of the data, highlight relationships, or the composition of the data? These questions will help you narrow your focus and decide which visualizations might be best for you to use to achieve your goal. Once you have this goal in mind, then you can start to narrow your focus regarding which graphs are going to fit this goal.

Traditional Graphs Versus Analytic Driven Visualizations

Statistical graphs are great at representing the data; however, some of the greatest insight is when this is combined with analytics to get a laser focus on what matters in the data. The best statistical graphs enrich the data and ensure that a more statistical insight is derived, and they show more than just counts and amounts. The traditional graphs in data visualizations simply display the data. They can have some dimensionality, but they are simply slicing or segmenting the data by known data elements.

More important than a pretty picture is your higher intent: generating insight.

Analytics-Driven Visualization

Adding analytics-driven visualization to your data visualizations and dashboards enables you to generate insight that is previously unavailable in your original data, unless you have skills to generate this using code. Using analytics can do two things, help you understand your data and how to best visualize it, and also generate insight that might end up being the main message of your data visualization. It is useful here to talk about some examples of what analytics underpinning the graphs can provide.

Word Cloud Versus Text Topics

A word cloud is often used in data visualizations to show the frequency of categories in a data table, and this can be useful to add value to the right data visualization project than using a bubble plot to show the same information. Take this a step further and use the word cloud as part of a self-service analysis underpinned by SAS Text Analytics. SAS derives topics being discussed inside these categories, which provides more insight. Using text analytics, we have enriched our original data set with additional insight as part of an analytic-driven visualization.

Figure 6.1 compares traditional world cloud versus an object driven by text analysis that includes derived topics. Document details and sentiment analysis provide insights that are not visible in the traditional word cloud graphic.

Figure 6.1: Traditional word cloud versus text topics (including a word cloud)

Word Cloud

Word Cloud Driven by Text Analytics

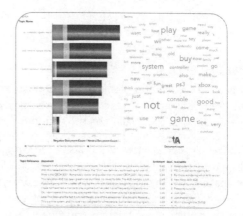

VS

Time Series Versus Forecast Object

A time series graph is a great way to represent the past performance of time-based data or trends and is useful for your traditional reporting and dashboards; however, in this era, we need to be doing things smarter, and the ability to look forward with a click of a mouse is important. SAS Visual Analytics includes a forecast object that is designed to use advanced analytics to forecast the performance yet to come from the data of the past, and the visual highlights the model data versus the actual performance of the past to assist with decision making and analysis.

Using time as a visual, you are connecting relative performance for your audience and providing a clear composition of the data for today or tomorrow, relative to the performance of the data last year or next year. Figure 6.2 shows the traditional time series plot versus a plot using analytics embedded. The visual allows the user to look at what might happen in the future, rather than just what occurred in the past.

Figure 6.2: Traditional time series versus forecasting object (including what if analysis)

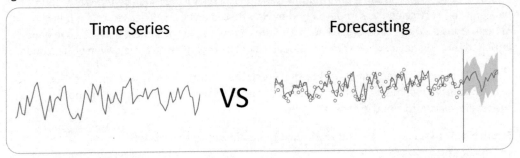

Parallel Coordinates Plot Versus Clustering and Segmentation

A parallel coordinates plot is a very powerful graph that maps each row in a data table as a line, and each attribute of the row is represented by a point along the line. It is useful for comparing many variables and visualizing the relationships and patterns within the data.

The parallel coordinates plot is also used within the composite graphs that are used when displaying the Cluster Analysis object within SAS Visual Analytics, and this is when the true power of analytics driving the visualization. This analytics-driven visualization highlights groups and segments within the data, and then displays these on a heat map and a parallel coordinates plot. However, this time the data is enriched with the segment/cluster ID, and this can be saved back into your data set to enable you to use the cluster id in another graph, like a pie chart or an object like a button bar filter. So, in this case, like so many in SAS Visual Analytics, you are uncovering patterns by using advanced analytics and enriching your original data with data derived from analytics. You are allowing the data science to show you groups within your data, not just relying on judgment and instinct.

Figure 6.3 shows a parallel coordinates plot versus an object driven by k-means analysis, which includes derived cluster IDs and provides insight that is not visible in the traditional parallel coordinates plot.

Figure 6.3: Parallel coordinates plot versus cluster (including a parallel coordinates plot)

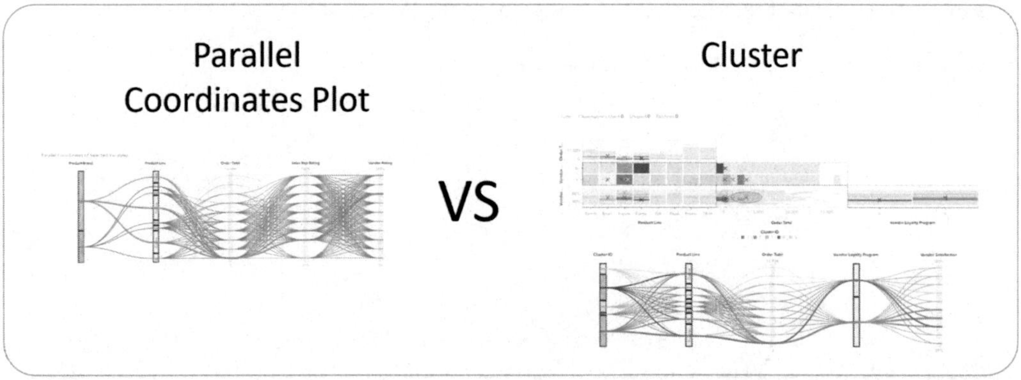

Basic Map Versus Location Intelligence

This scenario is unique because both the basic static map display and the location intelligence outlined here are included in the same geo map object in SAS Visual Analytics. Geo map graphs are a great visual as they can bring your data to life and anchor the data with familiar references – *location*. Placing data on a static map was ok in the past; however, today the expectation of the current end user is much more sophisticated. We can thank the rise of smart phones and apps for the increased user expectation around using technology and geospatial to get insight in an instant. Today, the map must add some additional value, not just display data. That is why SAS continues to work with geospatial providers such as Esri (a global leader in GIS) and continues to add features to enhance the data visualization experience with geospatial data. Location intelligence combines business data, geospatial data and analytics with mapping visualizations. It is this combination that enables users to visualize the "where" dimension in routes, patterns, trends, and other spatial relationships.

SAS has provided simple and advanced location analytics right inside SAS Visual Analytics, and this is surfaced to the user in multiple ways. Some of the integration include enriching your data with demographic and geospatial data sets that can be imported into SAS Visual Analytics from your relevant location of interest – yes, this means you can get data to enrich your existing data set. You could also provide elements like geospatial filters using live or historic traffic data, and feature searching from key geospatial features to combine the real world with your data. Automatic geo clusters are a great way to improve usability of large amount of location points in your data visualization. Lastly, display networks and route analysis overlay on a Geo Map to bring your network data to life.

Using location analytics is a great way to increase adoption of your reports and dashboards in SAS and can be a very familiar way for users to engage with data. Figure 6.4 shows a static map versus an enriched user experience by embedding location intelligence within the dashboard. It is a great way to increase the use and relevance of a data visualization. As the ability to zoom and interact with data that was not in the original data set is powerful for the end user.

Figure 6.4: Static map versus location intelligence

Map   Location Intelligence

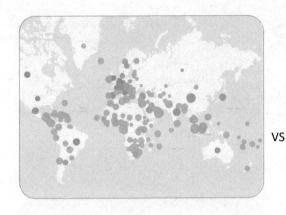 VS

Analytics are used throughout SAS Visual Analytics to uncover patterns and highlight anomalies, and there are many more analytic-driven visualizations than listed here. Analytics assist you to explore the data and derive value for your audience. This includes cutting edge machine learning models, model comparison, and much more, which can all be included within your dashboard if that helps tell the story with your data.

Traditional Graphs: Simple Yet Powerful

Traditional dashboards and data visualizations have graphs that are simple, yet powerful data-driven visual elements for your audience. There are many types of visualizations provided with SAS Visual Analytics that can highlight data in an instant and here are 10 high impact, yet approachable visualizations for use in your dashboards, in no particular order:

	Treemap – A treemap displays a hierarchy or a category as a set of rectangular tiles. It is a great graph to show large amounts of data, multidimensional (nested tiles) and multi-measure (color and size).
	Bar chart – A bar chart comprises vertical or horizontal bars that represent quantitative data. Use a small number of categories to best highlight comparative performance at a glance.

	Pie chart – A pie chart is widely used in reports and dashboards; some have said overused. It is a simple graph to show relative performance on a small number of categories. There are many graphs that may better fit your data, and be warned that your audience might not be able to see the difference in the slices of the pie, so use only in the right situation. By default, SAS Visual Analytics displays a pie chart as a donut chart because it is somewhat easier to differentiate slices in a donut chart. You can change this default in the object's options.
	Key value or KPI gauge – calling out important numbers is key. It is often useful to show a big number in your data visualization. Percentages and big numbers are useful here. Also, gauges are a great way to show actual versus target values at a glance.
	Correlation matrix or heat map – A correlation matrix displays the degree of correlation between multiple intersections of measures as a matrix. These are great to show relationships and highlight what matters from the data.
	Table – A table displays data as text. The data should be ranked top or bottom and fewer values is best. Sometimes more data is needed to tell the story; however, brevity is key with this visualization.
	Line graph – A line chart shows the relationship of one or more measures over some interval, such as time or a series of ranges. Timelines are brought to life with this graph, and it is a relatable way to see data for the viewer.
	Geo map – geospatial data is a favorite of many people because it can take the digital world and overlay it on the physical world. Maps offer instant familiarity.
	Network – A network diagram is composed of nodes (values) and links (relationships). It is popular to show relationships at a glance, which can lessen the time to insight.
	Word cloud – A word cloud displays a set of words from a character data item. Depending on the type of word cloud and your data, the size and color of each word in the cloud can indicate the numeric data. These are great for highlighting importance and relative performance using words. Alternatively, a bubble plot could be used if words do not work for your design.

Many more graph options are available depending on the story that needs to be told from your data. If you are like us, you might find one you use for a while, and then move onto another that may be more interesting to you and the audience.

Endless Graphing Options Within SAS Visual Analytics

Custom SAS Graphs

Custom SAS graphics are a great way to extend your functionality with SAS, and there are some great blogs and resources out on the internet. Use SAS Graph Builder to create combinations that only your imagination can design. One paper on the original custom graph feature created a graph named "the bubblefly chart," using elements of a bubble plot and butterfly chart (also known as the population pyramid) (Murphy 2015). You can take this a step further with the SAS code and unlock the power of SAS to craft the exact graphic to tell the desired story with your data. One SAS blog on this topic showed off how SAS can create pretty much any graph you can think of, like the circle graph, which connects related data with weighted lines across the circle (Matange 2016). Refer to the latest features from SAS Visual Analytics for all the options in creating custom graphs (SAS 2020b).

Third-Party Data-Driven Content

Innovators all over the globe are turning data into art. Some have increased complexity that is an example of form over function, whereby the challenge of the designer is maximum functionality while still being appealing.

You can now include these third-party visualizations in SAS Visual Analytics – and you can create and contribute these to the SAS community. Learn from others in the SAS community, and from other communities like D3 charts, chart.js, and other chart engines out on the internet, some open source and some proprietary. SAS Global Forum papers that highlight some of these options are a great place to start for trying out this endless extensibility with SAS.

More Than a Pretty Picture

Other objects and settings in SAS Visual Analytics can help refine your story, besides graphs, and can be just as important in the experience for your data visualization's audience. How the audience interacts with the data visualization is just as important as how visually appealing the data visualization is. You want them to "like" the aesthetic enough to use it; however, you need them to be able to "use" the dashboard, and that is where object elements like prompts and containers come in.

Objects worth mentioning to add value to your user's experience are:

- **Containers** – the container is probably the most important object in SAS Visual Analytics. It enables you to gain much more control over all objects placed inside the container – even nested containers. This is very important to create the experience and design your audience desires.

- **Prompt Controls** – user-defined prompts add slice-and-dice and self-service to your dashboard. This helps make a single data visualization useful to many users and also enhances the self-service nature of your dashboard.

- **Parameters** – add parameters to allow your audience to set their own context. This is a great way to make a single data visualization useful for multiple audiences. Setting the parameter value upon dashboard runtime ensures that the data visualization is relevant to the audience.

- **Hierarchies** – adding hierarchies can provide a logical navigation or drill path for the end user. These are so simple to create and edit in SAS with on-the-fly hierarchies.

Go Beyond Default Settings

Settings within the data visualization objects also provide a great deal of capability and flexibility for your dashboard design. As you get more familiar with SAS Visual Analytics, you can step outside your comfort zone and go past the default settings in your objects. Some settings that provide quick wins in your data visualizations are:

- **Conditional formatting** – use the conditions and business rules that your audience cares about to visually highlight the relevant events in the data. Exception highlights are a great tool to catch the attention of your audience to what matters within their data. In SAS Visual Analytics, these are achieved using display rules or including cell graphs into tables.

- **Animation** – set the animation role on many objects in SAS Visual Analytics. This will unlock animation over time, which is great way for users to interact with their data. Pressing a play button can be great to capture an executive audience, as they can see the data dance across the screen for time-based performance.

- **Alerts** – add alerting to the data to ensure the audience only needs to check the dashboard upon an event or exception occurring. Think of a warning light for engine oil versus checking the engine oil each time you get into the vehicle under the hood. Much more convenient for an executive.

- **Actions** – adding interactivity to a data visualization is so important today, and using the actions panel in SAS VA, you can make as much or as little interactivity as you desire. The "one-click" automatic filter option makes everything interactive and is a great way to supercharge your dashboards.

- **Drill Through** – add detail data behind your summary data visualization to help add value by giving the detail behind the pictures. The ability to use hidden pages in SAS provides a flexible landing page for your drill-through actions and provides context filtering from the source to target automatically.

Conclusion

Remember your driving principle: the message that you want to tell with your data visualization. As you progress throughout your design, all objects and settings that you use need to stay true to the original message. This can become feature over functionality quickly, and as the data visualization designer, do not forget that your responsibility is to your audience. Clarity of message is key, and generating useful and timely insight should mean your dashboard or data visualization resonates and is popular with your audience. Keep on checking with your audience and refine the design over time and continue to make the information actionable. Happy designing! Please reach out via the SAS Visual Analytics Communities to share your stories or ask questions.

References

Matange, Sanjay. 2016. "Outside-the-box: Directed circle link graphs." SAS Blog: Graphically Speaking. November 1, 2016.
https://blogs.sas.com/content/graphicallyspeaking/2016/11/01/outside-box-directed-circle-link-graphs/

McCandless, David. 2010. "The beauty of data visualization." Filmed in July 2010 at TEDGlobal 2010. Video 17:42
https://www.ted.com/talks/david_mccandless_the_beauty_of_data_visualization

Murphy, Travis. 2015. "How to Tell the Best Story with Your Data Using SAS® Visual Analytics Graph Builder." Proceedings of the SAS® Global Forum 2015 Conference. Cary, NC: SAS Institute Inc. .
https://support.sas.com/resources/papers/proceedings15/SAS1800-2015.pdf

Murphy, Travis. 2018. *Infographics Powered by SAS®: Data Visualization Techniques for Business Reporting.* Cary, NC: SAS Institute Inc.

SAS. 2020a. "Creating Accessible Reports Using SAS® Visual Analytics 8.5." *SAS.com*, June 12, 2020.
https://documentation.sas.com/?cdcId=vacdc&cdcVersion=8.5&docsetId=vacar&docsetTarget=titlepage.htm

SAS. 2020b. "Documentation: Find user's guides and other technical documentation for SAS Visual Analytics."
https://support.sas.com/en/software/visual-analytics-support.html#documentation

SAS n.d. "SAS Visual Analytics Community." Accessed on August 1, 2020. https://communities.sas.com/t5/SAS-Visual-Analytics/bd-p/sas_va

Chapter 7: Creation Process

Overview

This chapter aims to provide ideas around a repeatable approach for creating data journeys with your dashboards in SAS Visual Analytics. Think of this as a data visualization creation process. Focusing on steps in the process can make your project run smoothly and improve the impact your data visualization will have with your audience.

Audience

This is a general topic that outlines a process for all SAS users to follow and will provide ideas for all readers. Business teams can see how they can clearly layout their requirements and hand these off to analysts for faster insights and more impact from each data project.

> *"The greatest value of a picture is when it forces us to notice what we never expected to see."*
>
> *John Tukey*

Introduction

We rely on processes to help perform and maintain consistency in many tasks that we attempt and complete each day. In data operations and analytics this is also true. Creating data visualizations is more freeform than many other data projects because it combines both art and science. This mix between creativity and productivity requires some process steps to support speed, accuracy, and quality outcomes.

Approach Patterns

All analysts have different approaches to data visualization projects and dashboard creation. The following are some styles we have observed working with others on data projects in the past:

- **Play** – just wing it! Luckily, SAS has your back here as you can use SAS Visual Analytics to change the graph and use the build-in automatic chart creation feature to see if the data tells the correct story and the latest suggestions pane using to get some inspiration.

- **Have a plan** – sketch out your data visualization design and ask questions like, is the data ready for display, can I highlight the data better, and is the whole data visualization balanced?

- **Consensus wins** – discuss what others would like to see and how others have solved this before. Using sites like Google Images and Pinterest is a great way to see other examples of the data and how it has been represented.

These approaches are neither right or wrong and will all result in a finished project. However, we find that a combination of these approaches is best. We have included elements of each at various stages of the design process.

Approaching Your Data Visualization Project

This chapter is intended to share the approach that we use to create data visualizations and provide a repeatable template for you to try on your own project. The creation process is often very personal; however, we have found that working together for many years and collaborating on projects, our shared process developed, and we have approached our own projects in similar ways. As outlined, this approach is flexible and allows for creating and exploration.

Approaching any data visualization design project almost always requires a non-technical approach: a pen and paper. As outlined in the paper presented at SAS Global Forum 2018, we introduced a repeatable data visualization creation process design, tools, and output (Murphy and Schulz 2018). We use these ideas before embarking on any dashboard or data visualization project, and each of these decisions can impact the success of your project. Let's discuss these steps briefly as we apply these decisions to frame our data visualization scope.

When starting out, it is important to keep in mind the following elements when designing and building data visualizations. Each element is important and can impact the success of the final product.

The Process

You might have read about our process in previous examples and publications about our design of infographics and dashboards. This section recaps it once to show how we approach designing data visualization projects (Figure 7.1).

Figure 7.1: The design process (Murphy and Schulz 2018)

The design – What question are you answering? When designing a dashboard with infographic inspirations, it is recommended to you to start with a whiteboard or pen and paper. This step takes the analyst out of a tools frame of mind and removes constraints on your design. You will sketch out a design that tells the story that you want to tell, and not what the software tools allow you to tell. That will come next.

The tools – the tool that you choose will have an impact on what you can achieve, and if your design is possible at all. We all have amazing aspirations in our original design stage, which cannot always be fully achieved in tools we can use. When using SAS Visual Analytics, we can achieve flexible designs including analytical visuals versus traditional data visualization elements.

The output – The display and consumption of the data visualization is very important and will impact the way you build and implement your design. If you are planning to use this visualization one time only and then share a static version of the report, then you do not have to think too hard about the performance and repeatability or real-time interactions. If you know your audience will use this as their analytics application to slice and dice all data combinations, then you must design for usability also.

Workflow for Building Your Data Visualization with SAS Visual Analytics

Having a simple workflow is important to creating a dashboard for impact. Combining your creativity with the following steps will produce impressive results to inspire your audience on your next project.

Topic

You need to have a question to answer or topic to explore at the outset. Some data preparation might be needed at this step to load or transform the data and conduct some exploratory analysis to understand what insight may be available to uncover and share. This step is where you can take an initial look at the data, start to explore, and discover what may be useful (Figure 7.2).

Figure 7.2: SAS Visual Analytics data prep – data uncovers a story or a point of view

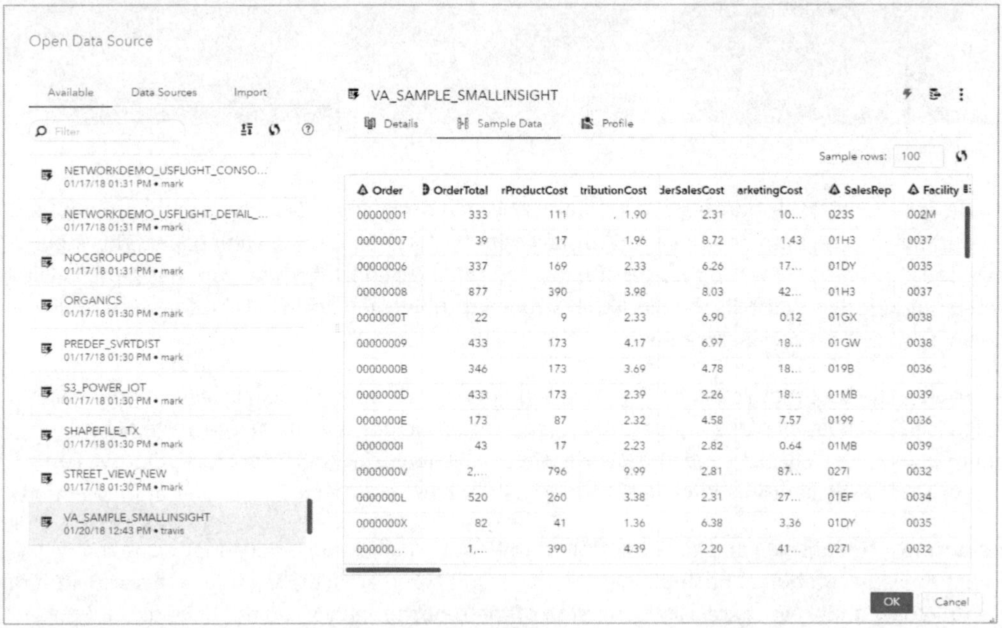

Design

We always need to think about the general design of the data visualization – use pen and paper or a whiteboard to start to lay out the design. You can bring the ideas out a bit more easily than sitting at the keyboard trying to make magic happen with mouse clicks. Give yourself some space to think about how this might look and place yourself in your audience's position.

As shown in Figure 7.3, we always start with a mockup of the design. This helps understand how many data visualizations or dashboard pages are needed to tell the complete story on the topic you have decided to cover.

Figure 7.3: Example mockup of a data visualization design

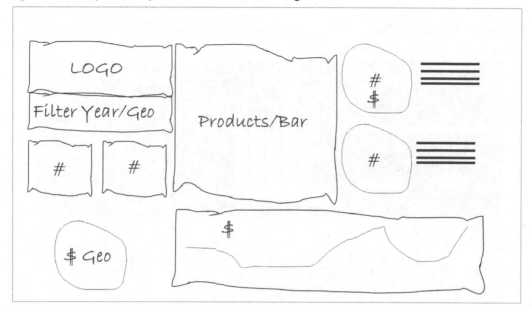

Build

Using the tools, in this case SAS Visual Analytics, we will build out the data visualization and refine the design throughout the build (Figure 7.4). Formatting data visualizations to the point where they are looking like infographics goes against the principle of simple and automatic layouts for use across any device or platform. This is not dissimilar to desktop publishing where you have the output in mind and a clear vision of the way this will be consumed. When building your data visualization with highly formatted design, you need to consider how you plan to consume or deploy the final output.

Figure 7.4: SAS Visual Analytics – a powerful toolset to design visually rich visualizations (Murphy 2020)

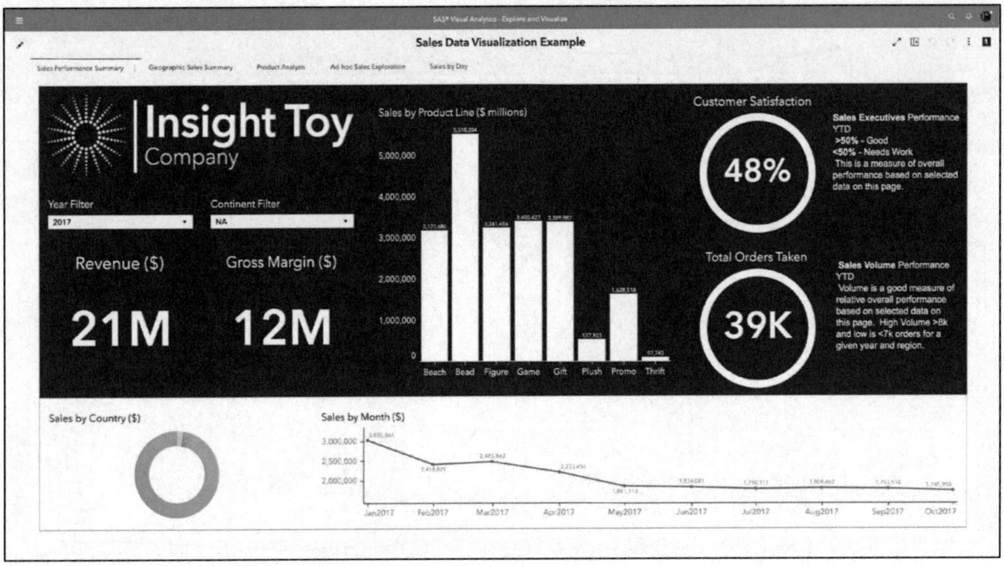

Final Tips for Data Visualization Projects

Before you finish your visualization project, you should confirm the following checklist to ensure that your dashboard or data visualization is ready for sharing. These checks will make so much difference in the final result.

- **Confirm Audience** – Be specific. For example, general public versus management.

- **Simplicity** – Minimize number of visual types and use the most simplified representation (for example, KPI versus list table). If you have content for multiple stories, then chances are you need more than one infographic.

- **Focus** – Apply techniques to draw attention to the key areas. Stay on one topic or story.

- **Headline** – Design it as big and bold statement. Use a short but descriptive banner text or graphic.

- **Balance** – Use both information and graphics to tell your story with the weight on the visuals.

- **Art** – Get creative. Use white space. Use story-matching "simple" color themes. Decide on a consistent font style.

- **Flow** – The audience starts at the headline then works its way through all of the linked visuals.

- **Recheck the facts** – Obvious one. Double-check all of the facts and sources.

- **Cite** – Be sure to cite sources and include a footer with author details.

Conclusion

There are many rigid steps that we could outline; however, we have found that sticking to these steps is enough structure to get a great result. Also, too much structure can stifle creativity, which is so important in data visualization design. We are always looking for ideas to improve our process, but we always come back to these simple steps. Artistic expression is so important in the modern data project, and when combined with ideas in this chapter, your data visualization will have the desired impact with your audience. In Part 2 of this book, we apply these approaches to create impactful data visualizations with some open data to show these steps in process supporting real world examples.

References

Murphy, Travis and Falko Schulz. 2018. "Supercharge Your Dashboards with Infographic Concepts Using SAS® Visual Analytics." In Proceedings of the SAS® Global Forum 2018 Conference. Cary, NC: SAS Institute Inc.https://www.sas.com/content/dam/SAS/support/en/sas-global-forum-proceedings/2018/2069-2018.pdf

Murphy, Travis. 2020. "Create Impactful Data Journeys for "Informavores" with SAS® Visual Analytics on SAS® Viya®" In Proceedings of the SAS® Global Forum 2020 Conference. Cary, NC: SAS Institute Inc. https://www.sas.com/content/dam/SAS/support/en/sas-global-forum-proceedings/2020/4158-2020.pdf

Tukey, John W. 1977. *Exploratory Data Analysis*. Reading, MA: Addison-Wesley.

Part 2: In Practice

In **Part 2**, we discuss the software used in this book and step through examples of creating impactful dashboards and data visualizations with SAS. We demonstrate how to use your software from accessing data all the way through to sharing your data visualization designs. You will be given various software tips and best practices to inspire you.

Chapter 8: Data Holds the Answers

Overview

Data holds the answers to questions that we have today and possible outcomes for our future. The importance of data and how you access, process, and analyze it is the language of modern society. Skills required to perform data analysis range dramatically depending on the tools you have available. Better data management leads to better analytics, and this chapter will look at this further.

Audience

This chapter has a little bit of something for everyone who needs data. It discusses the various options that SAS Visual Analytics and SAS Viya provide users to work with data.

> *"There are data in every aspect of our lives, every aspect of work and pleasure, and it's not just about the number of places where data comes, it's about connecting it."*

Tim Berners-Lee

Introduction

As the above quote describes, data is everywhere, and the value is when you combine and connect data to create insight. The examples in this book use various techniques and features to get data from different sources and access it using SAS Viya. This chapter steps through the options that are available in SAS Viya so that we can highlight the many big data approaches that you have at your fingertips. We step through specific options for the creation of the examples in later chapters. Remember when you are starting your dashboard or data visualization project, everything starts with a question and the data answers these questions.

Data Is Everywhere

The resurgence of coders today has happened for many reasons. One of these reasons is the availability of data and access to that data. The data is available everywhere, and organizations are struggling to effectively stage and manage all of this data at the speed at which it is coming. New sources are created all the time, and with an open data strategy being used by many research and governments across the globe, curated and trusted data sources continue to rise. Often, the only way to access these data streams is via web APIs, which by their nature are unique to the source and its structure and require some coding to get efficient access to the source. Not everything is in a spreadsheet ready for the traditional desktop analyst.

Coders are often the people who have whipped the data sources into shape for release as they build in rules and routines to cleanse and analyze the raw files to create a curated view of the source files. This is where the coder is providing another data file for their audience, often other coders or analysts who expect nice, clean data. The more hands this data goes through, the more obfuscated it becomes from the original sources. This is not always a bad thing, as many data sets are then merged with other important data views for a much richer perspective for analysts. Obfuscation is also what often protects us from privacy breaches of personal data being leaked across the world.

Data is the first step in the analytics life cycle, and the journey starts and ends with data. Data is also leveraged by all users in business today, from business analysts to data scientists. Research and our own experience tell us that organizations often spend 80 percent of their team's time working on data preparation or validation when trying to deliver analytics projects. SAS can analyze data of any complexity, speed, and size, whether it is traditional structured data or a new format such as streaming sensor data. We believe data should never be a limit to your analytics. SAS Viya provides a robust suite of data management tools but also work seamlessly with other data management products on the market (SAS 2020).

As mentioned, data preparation is estimated to take up to 80 percent of the time spent on an analytics project. That is time that can be better spent building models and dashboards. SAS Viya streamlines data preparation with native access engines, integrated data quality, and data preparation tools that leverage artificial intelligence to automate time consuming tasks. This makes it easy to create and monitor high quality analytic ready data.

Preparing Data for Dashboards

Combining data is often the thing that advanced analytics and reporting tools are not able to accomplish well. SAS Visual Analytics has data preparation built right into the same tool and provides simple to advanced features depending on the skills of the analyst or complexity of the task. Users have many options for data preparation with SAS.

There is a plethora of modern options when doing data preparation and data mashups with SAS Viya. You can code in SAS or open source, you can use the SAS prepare data tools with visual drag and drop, or you can just drag and drop your spreadsheets directly onto your dashboards and get started right away. The following are some of these options that we use in our data projects.

Data Exploration

If you are new to SAS Viya or deal with unknown data sources, one of the best places to learn about the data content, its structure, and related profile is the data exploration interface accessible from within SAS Environment Manager and other applications (Figure 8.1). Not only can you quickly import data of any kind, but you can also explore sample data and create data profiles.

Figure 8.1: SAS Environment Manager – data management

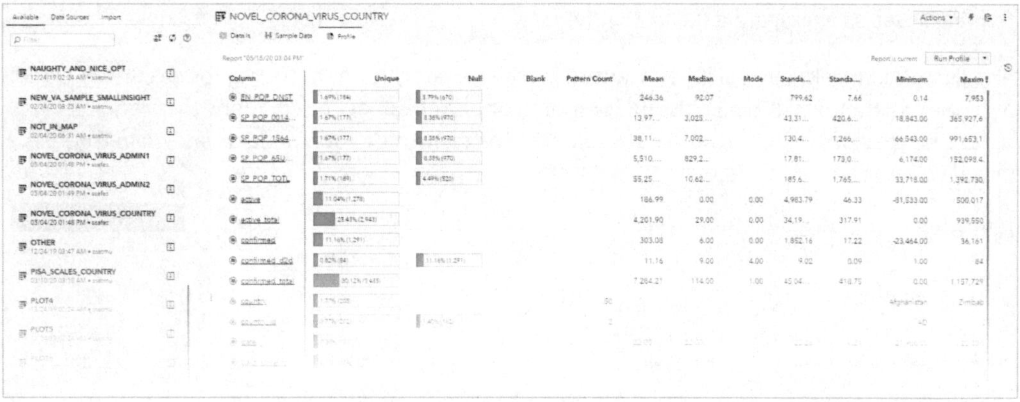

The profiling results provide great insights about the data structure. From statistics like number of null or missing values to common measures such as minimum, maximum, or average values. Understanding your data source is a key step in decided on next steps to prepare your data for visualization. You are also able to import new data into the environment. If you have local data sources such as comma-separated files or Microsoft Excel spreadsheets, you can simply drop items into this interface for automated import. If data is already stored in other RDBMS databases, you will be able to create related data connections and read data directly in SAS Viya.

TIP: Geospatial Data Enrichment

Data often comes with location-based information. Think about common information like customer address fields such as street, city, or postal code. Given such information you can also apply built-in geo encoding and enrichment processes. This is useful for data visualization later because you can map information on geographical maps along with additional demographic information. Note that this data transformation technique requires access to Esri ArcGIS premium services and related ArcGIS Online account (as seen in the figure on the right).

SAS Visual Analytics

Besides SAS Visual Analytics being the main discovery and visualization tool, SAS Visual Analytics also has some basic data preparation tools built in. A task often performed is to join multiple data sources given a common identifier. In the past, you had to go into special data management tools to do so. Depending on the situation and data complexity, SAS Visual Analytics enables you to join as well as aggregate data on the fly.

An aggregation task is useful if you want to pre-aggregate your data source for easier calculation and role assignments. It is also useful for more complex business calculations that require different types of pre-aggregated data sources. The same data tool menu as shown in Figure 8.2 provides access to "data views."

Figure 8.2: Visual Analytics data tools

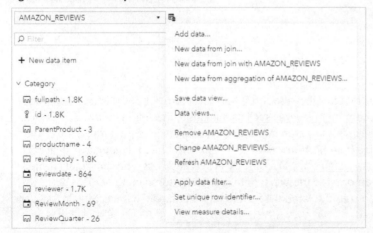

If you have spent a lot of time in the Data pane in order to prepare related data items for reporting – for instance, renaming columns, creating calculated fields, or even adding common data filters – being able to save this as re-usable data view is important. It will enable you to save your work and not only provide a quick entry into new reports but also share your work with others.

SAS Data Studio

If you need more complex data processing tools, the SAS Data Studio interface can help. It goes beyond standard data joins and filters and provides more advanced SQL-based transformation tools from simple calculations and filters to unusual matches or cluster analysis. You will also find options to append data to existing tables or simply join tables on common key columns.

Designed as a graphical user interface (GUI) for managing processes with drag-and-drop functionality, many of the tasks that required coding before can simply be designed in this interface and saved as re-usable data plan. You can also take advantage of common models applied to related data sources. Many AI and machine learning processes require data tables in a particular structure and format (for example, binary data instead of character fields). Data Studio enables you to apply such models without the need of writing a single line of code (Figure 8.3).

Figure 8.3: Data preparation models in SAS Data Studio

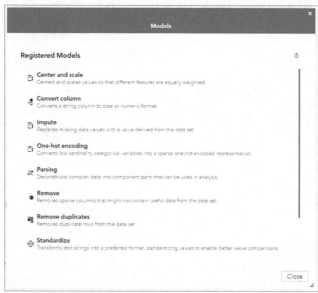

If you do not know which model to apply given your data tables, you may also try out the provided suggestions. A machine learning recommendation engine will scan your data source and suggest suitable transformations (Figure 8.4). Further, if you need access to the SAS code generated, you can also download the auto-generated code and apply further tweaks and edits using SAS Studio. This also leads us to the introduction of our final tool suitable for data preparation – targeting the coder.

Figure 8.4: Data transformations

SAS Studio

To transform your data, you can use SAS Studio. SAS Studio is a development environment for SAS that you access through your web browser. With SAS Studio, you can access your data files, libraries, and existing programs, and you can write new programs. Use the Program Editor in SAS Studio to write SAS DATA steps and use CAS actions to transform your data. To get started quickly, you can use existing code snippets. SAS Studio also supports version control with an integrated Git repository. We have used SAS Studio for various projects as well as some of the examples in the book. Some data sources have very unusual structures and having the freedom to massage the data using code provides great flexibility.

TIP: Desktop Options

Instead of using SAS Studio, you might prefer a desktop tool like SAS Enterprise Guide that now also supports SAS Viya. It is a popular user interface for SAS users across the globe.

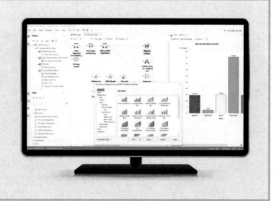

Agile Versus Production Data Processes

The options outlined here support both agile data preparation and production data processes. The benefit with SAS Viya is that you can allow the users to work with data in all situations and use cases and administrators can use simple drag-and-drop options, schedule jobs, and move these data processes from development to production in an instant. Not all data projects are elevated to production state; however, we recognize how important innovation and discovery is for an organization to identify opportunities in the data and move this quickly to support business operations. Often, the most impactful outcomes in production started as an experiment or discovery from the analyst in an agile process first.

Conclusion

As you have seen here, there are many ways to work with data in SAS Viya and often it depends on the user's skills and the complexity of the data that you are working with. Whether you are doing business intelligence or artificial intelligence, SAS Viya has you covered for all your data challenges. In the following chapters, we will use various techniques for each dashboard example. We acknowledge that our examples only touch on the data options in SAS Viya, so if your data project requires some different approaches, then try some of the data options outlined in this chapter and take advantage of SAS Viya to make your life a little easier.

References

Berners-Lee, Tim. 2009. "The next web." Filmed February 2009 at TED2009, Video, 15:52.
https://www.ted.com/talks/tim_berners_lee_the_next_web.

SAS. 2020. "SAS® DATA MANAGEMENT: Take charge of your data with the industry's leading integration technology." SAS.com. Accessed August 1, 2020. https://www.sas.com/en_us/software/data-management.html

Chapter 9: Examples Overview

Overview

This chapter provides an overview of the approach for the working examples that enable you to create insightful data visualizations with SAS Visual Analytics. All files are available for you to step yourself through these scenarios on your own time.

Audience

All SAS users will be provided with options and overview of examples in this chapter. You will move through basic, intermediate, and advanced SAS skills with each example. There is something for everyone in the following working examples.

> *"The goal is to turn data into information, and information into insight."*

Carly Fiorina

Introduction

This short chapter introduces the next part of the book where you get your hands on SAS Visual Analytics and start to build the examples that can help with your own data in your work environment. You will be leveraging the software outlined in the previous chapters to create a combination of data-driven graphics in the SAS software tools and subjective content in order to build dashboards with SAS Visual Analytics and SAS code.

General Structure of Examples

The Three Is of Visualization model that we outlined in Chapter 2 shows that the two perspectives of audience and analyst are related and are a way to frame the effort required to get value from the visualizations. The following examples are designed with the analyst in mind as we are creating the data journey with our audience as the end user. The steps of each example are laid out in Figure 9.1, and you can see the general construct of how we will step through each example from INFORM, INSIGHT, to INSPIRE.

Figure 9.1: Simplified three-I model – simple layout to anchor steps in the how-to examples

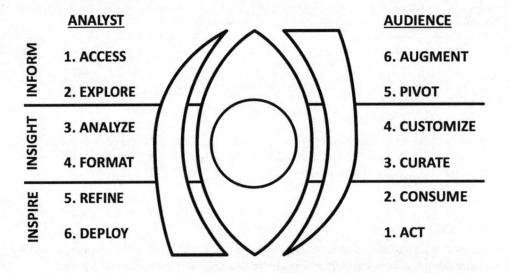

This means that as the analyst, we will approach the project examples from your perspective. Later in the book in Chapter 13, we look at the options the audience has in more detail.

Data

We have chosen to use open data in all the examples in this book. This decision was a conscious one because we realize that the explosion of open data over recent years has provided a fantastic resource for both analysts and audiences to answer questions like never before. The open data sources are selected for a variety of reasons, including interest level to most people, legal permission to use this the data in a book like this, and topics that are rich and interesting to share in a comprehensive data journey via the dashboards. That said, open data has a habit of changing in availability and structure over time: what was there today is not always there tomorrow.

So, the caveat that we include here is that the data and projects were all working at the time the book was published. Of course, we will attempt to keep the sample files up-to-date based on your feedback, so please let us know if the data imports or samples do not work and we will endeavor to revisit if possible.

Having worked on many open data portals for customers over the years, we hope that these examples encourage others to build useful visualizations with the open data and ensure all analysts and audience have options to engage with the data in the future.

Topics

The following are the included examples that are in the chapters to follow:

- **SAS and Social Media Data** – combining the power of SAS with data pulled from social media information provided in tweets, we step through the data, design, and build of a social media dashboard.

- **SAS and Climate Data** – global warming is brought to life in the example where we combine SAS and global weather data to build an infographic style-visualization for weather.

- **SAS and Outbreak Data** – given the impact of COVID-19 and the popularity of the SAS Visual Analytics dashboard provided throughout the pandemic, we step through an example of building a dashboard to assist situational awareness during a health crisis.

Tools

The following tools are required to start the process to create inspirational dashboards and data visualizations:

- **SAS software** – access to SAS Visual Analytics on SAS Viya – this can be at your office or using the free online software trial (SAS 2020).

- **Internet browser** – we have provided many resources in this book to augment the examples we step through. Please use these videos, blogs, and user guide links to enhance your experience for anything we do not cover in detail.

- **Enthusiasm and patience** – open data, highly formatted designs, and new concepts can be frustrating until you get the hang of it all. We are relying on your enthusiasm to keep yourself following the examples and trying things out for yourself.

Conclusion

Let's jump right into SAS Visual Analytics and follow along with each example, step-by-step, and pull some inspiration for your next dashboard project. Each example includes SAS files that are provided for reference and educational purposes. These are not production-tested solutions and are included as companions to this book. As mentioned, examples are based on open data available on the internet. The examples were selected for their interest to the authors and projects that will highlight the use of SAS solutions. The data processing steps and code are made available for you to follow along or re-create these on your own SAS environments. The dashboards and visualizations and other files like images are made available to assist with the learning and benefit of the reader. For samples and more from the authors, please visit the authors' pages at https://support.sas.com/en/books/authors/falko-schulz.html and https://support.sas.com/en/books/authors/travis-murphy.html.

References

Fiorina, Carly. 2004. "Information: the currency of the digital age." Speech at Oracle OpenWorld – San Francisco. December 6, 2004. http://www.hp.com/hpinfo/execteam/speeches/fiorina/04openworld.html

SAS. 2020. "FREE SOFTWARE TRIALS: Discover how SAS® helps you explore, analyze and visualize your data." https://www.sas.com/en_us/trials.html

Chapter 10: Example 1: SAS and Social Media Data

Overview

This chapter steps through an example using SAS with open data from the internet. We will step through the process of accessing data from publicly available websites. Open-data scraping is a popular technique for analysts today and opens a world of possibility to practice skills and augment other data sets that are in use for your analysis.

Audience

This example is for an intermediate SAS user. The steps can be followed by any user with skills in data analysis and data structures; however, anyone can follow along with this to further understand the capabilities in SAS Visual Analytics on SAS Viya.

> *"Social networks are these intricate things of beauty, and they're so elaborate and so complex and so ubiquitous that one has to ask what purpose they serve."*

Nicholas Christakis

Introduction

Today, we have so many rich and expansive data sources that are available to help all businesses understand their customers and their place in the world. The speed at which users adopt online tools, like social media, has created vast and ever-growing data sets to provide businesses with insight that they would have needed to pay expensive consultancy companies or market research firms for in the past. Data-rich open platforms like Twitter, Facebook, website analytics, blogs, forums, and many more are now available for you and your organization to benefit from.

Open data, including government research on health, welfare, economics, safety, traffic, and many more services, are now provided for all to use and analyze. The power of one data set is great on its own; however, this is multiplied when you can merge and enrich one from another to provide a clearer picture and insight that you thought was never possible. This can be as simple as using the geographic data in one service, combined with geographic demographics in another source to understand and uncover patterns not in either data set initially.

This example uses Twitter data. We all know the global impact that Twitter has had on the world, both socially and politically, since its creation in 2006 by creator Jack Dorsey (Wikipedia 2020). Like all rich data, looking at a single tweet provides you a single point of view, versus looking at all tweets in a data set where it provides you a narrative that otherwise was obscured in all the detailed data. This example steps through the stages of creating impact from Twitter data and provide a repeatable approach to accessing any open data on the internet using application programming interfaces (APIs) and SAS.

Project Approach

Decisions that we make at the beginning of any analysis will often enable or restrict what we can include in our data visualization later down the path. It is important at this stage to have your most inclusive perspective possible because we can always remove and refine as we look to support our data processes in a production phase. We are in an exploratory stage, so the richness and flexibility of the data matters. Each data element is important and will impact the success of the final product. This is often why on a data warehouse project when we sit with our users and stakeholders and we ask what they want by column and row, they say, "We want all the data!" At this early stage in the process, many questions are not even formed. The data needs to be explored and understood to start to define what is available and, therefore, what is even possible.

So, the general approach with this project is to scrape SAS Global Forum Twitter data from the internet. SAS Global Forum is the premier user's conference for SAS software users around the world. This event generates Twitter activity for attendees and non-attendees across the entire SAS community. Once we scrape the data, we will explore the relationship of tweets and attributes of the tweets. These attributes include location, retweets, topics, and time of the tweets. We will uncover patterns in the data and look at the best visualizations to communicate these insights. This project will show what is possible for your own organization's Twitter data.

Preparation is more than just having your data prepared. You need to understand some of the key elements of your overall project. Here we rely on answering our standard key questions:

The design – Initial dashboard page design mock-ups should reflect our audience who are internal marketing stakeholders, who are not programmers, and who want to understand more about our network and impact on social media. We will need a comprehensive suite of outputs to support multiple desired audiences.

The tools – Selected software tools that we are working with are SAS Visual Analytics and SAS Studio to connect to the APIs and build the data set over time.

The output – Most of the users will be interacting with our outputs for dashboards online inside of SAS Visual Analytics. We know our aim here is to create many visual elements for different audiences, so we will work from data outputs, to dashboards, and to infographic posters within this project. The output for this example is a dashboard with interactivity and a large poster for sharing on high-resolution printers.

INFORM

ACCESS

Like many open data sources, gaining value from Twitter data is very easy because we get many standard metrics to analyze quickly. Twitter-specific elements such as likes and retweets metrics can tell a powerful story on their own. Importantly, Twitter data helps to describe behavior, relationships, and location, which enriches our understanding of the data.

Twitter is becoming an important data source for organizations who want to better understand customer feedback on social channels. Before you can analyze Twitter data, however, you will need to import tweets and user profiles into SAS. For this example, data has been downloaded daily over a period of time using Twitter's public API (Twitter 2020). A SAS data job has been developed to call API endpoints to crawl each day's tweets and add them to the master data table. Data is typically downloaded in JSON format and added to a SAS data table. SAS provides a convenient JSON LIBNAME statement here to automatically map JSON files (Schulz 2013).

Steps required to access Twitter API:

1. You must have a Twitter app to generate your access tokens. Twitter apps can be registered using the Twitter developer portal. You must have an approved developer account to create a Twitter app.
2. The developer portal allows generating access tokens for a given application.
3. Using the generated access token and access token secret, an authorization token can be requested. That is typically done as first step in your crawler job. Every corresponding API endpoint request will need to carry this authorization token.

The daily crawler job used for this example covers the following steps:

1. Request Twitter API authorization token using access token and secret.
2. Validate existing SAS detail tables. Create tables if required.
3. Execute a Twitter API search request given query arguments (for example, filter-specific hashtags or user profiles).
4. Import JSON file into SAS using the JSON LIBNAME statement.
5. Append new tweet information to the master tables.
6. Perform geocoding on newly added user profiles.
7. Pre-calculate network metrics.

Accessing APIs using SAS is very powerful, and you can benefit from many tools available to help you in the process. From the ability to execute a REST call (PROC HTTP) to reading JSON files, each will help to minimize the effort when communicating with API endpoints.

Reading JSON Data

SAS provides a convenient method to read JSON data. The JSON LIBNAME statement enables you to map an external file and import data straight into SAS data tables. A very basic example of such statement is as follows:

```
FILENAME infile "C:\Temp\tweets.json";
LIBNAME tweets JSON fileref=infile;
```

This code snippet imports the referenced JSON file into SAS using the default mappings. If the JSON file has a more complex or unusual structure, you can also provide a related mapping file. See the SAS documentation for more details about working with JSON files.

OAuth2 authorization

Being able to authenticate to 3rd party API providers is very important and required for most of the endpoints. Understanding how OAuth2 authorization works and what steps are required will be important for any API developer. Also note that while we use Twitter API as example here, the same technique applies to other REST providers (for example, Facebook.).

Twitter supports authentication methods such as OAuth signed and application-only authentication. Both methods use access tokens and token secrets in order to authenticate with Twitter API. We will focus on the application-only authentication method. Twitter supports authenticating on behalf of the application itself (as opposed to on behalf of a specific user). This means that there will not be a user context and you will not have access to endpoints such as POST statuses or updates. On the other hand, this authentication method is simpler and sufficient for popular tasks such as tweet searches.

The following code snippet shows how to obtain the bearer token:

```
%let CONSUMER_KEY=<access_token>;
%let CONSUME_SECRET=<access_token_secret>;
%let JSON_TWEET_FILE=ResponseContent.txt;

/* Create a temporary file name used for the XMLMap */
%macro tempFile( fname );
  %if %superq(SYSSCPL) eq %str(z/OS) or %superq(SYSSCPL) eq %str(OS/390)
%then
    %let recfm=recfm=vb;
  %else
    %let recfm=;
  filename &fname TEMP lrecl=2048 &recfm;
%mend;

/* create temp files for the content and header input streams */
%tempFile(in);
%tempFile(hdrin);

/* keep the response permanently */
filename out "&JSON_TWEET_FILE.";

/* post request content is the grant_type */
data _null_;
   file in;
   put "grant_type=client_credentials&";
run;

/* request the bearer token by providing consumer key and secret */
data _null_;
     file hdrin;
     consumerKey = urlencode("&CONSUMER_KEY.");
     consumerSecret = urlencode("&CONSUME_SECRET.");
     encodedAccessToken  = put( compress(consumerKey || ":" ||
consumerSecret),$base64x32767.);
     put "Authorization: Basic " encodedAccessToken;
run;

proc http method="post"
    in=in out=out
      headerin=hdrin
    url="https://api.twitter.com/oauth2/token"
    ct="application/x-www-form-urlencoded;charset=UTF-8";
run;

/* Store bearer token in macro variable */
libname token json fileref=out;
```

```
proc sql noprint;
      select value into: BEARER_TOKEN
      from token.alldata
      where p1 eq "access_token";
quit;run;
%put BEARER_TOKEN: &BEARER_TOKEN;
libname token;
```

The code snippet above shows how to communicate with Twitter API and request an access token. More details and a full example can be found on the SAS Voices blog (Schulz 2013).

Transform and Enrich Data

Additional data transformation was added to calculate network metrics along with geographic enrichment (for example, the users' location). The data job also performed geocoding based on user profile information to determine the related geographic location. The location information will be used later in the visualization tool to produce useful geographical maps to show user distribution across the globe. These powerful data enrichment steps take advantage of some raw data elements in the Twitter data and leverage core capabilities of SAS for calculating network analytics metrics and geocoding for additional context.

These steps can be seen in Figure 10.1 using the feature-rich IDE with SAS Studio. This shows a sample transformation applied to the master table to extract tweets in a particular period for further analysis in SAS Viya. Please refer to the samples provided to see how you can leverage this in your next data process with SAS.

Figure 10.1: SAS Studio – SAS code is a powerful toolset to automate your processes

NOTE: SAS Studio – Save and Share your Code

SAS Studio enables you to save some or all of the code as a reusable snippet or even spend the time to create a code template for sharing with your whole team. There are so many powerful features for the enterprise using a visual code editor like SAS Studio.

For more information about the features of SAS Studio, refer to https://www.sas.com/en_us/software/studio.html.

EXPLORE

To get the best understanding from the data, we created a few sample visualizations to explore. Exploring the data source provides a quick and often rough understanding about tweet frequency and geographical distribution of people tweeting within our selected Twittersphere.

Figure 10.2: Data exploration – learning what the data holds

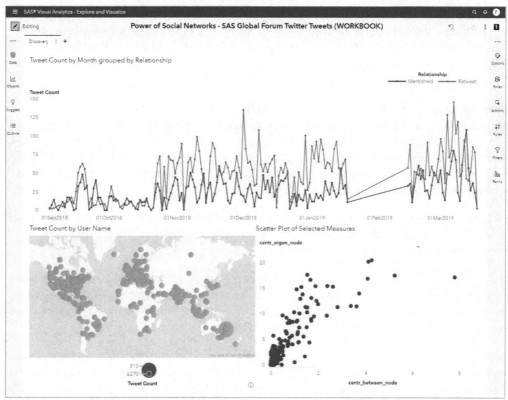

As seen in Figure 10.2, what you quickly see is that the tweet crawler data job stopped for a few weeks back in February due to a system failure. This highlights what data visualization explorations are good for – making sure one can validate data source and quality. This simple-to-create analysis brings the data to life and allows the analyst to see what is under the surface.

This is often the start of understanding what the audience would find interesting and useful in sharing this further. We are now starting on a path toward interpretation through discovery.

INSIGHT

ANALYZE

During this next step, we look to gain more insight into this enriched Twitter data set and provide insight that was not previously visible. Some of these steps have been a progression from the previous step, and others are unlocked due to the self-service analytics features delivered by SAS Visual Analytics. We are using a different lens, an analytical lens, which extends the methods we previously used to gain insight into this data.

Given the list of tweets, the Twitter API also enables you to add information about users mentioned in tweets as well as tweets being re-tweeted by others. This creates an interesting relationship between people tweeting and people consuming such tweets. As a result, such data can be visualized using network plots or further analyzed using SAS Viya to determine key actors and user's location within such network structure. You can find more information about social network analysis on the SAS Voices blog (Schulz 2014).

Additional steps for analysis may include segmentation based on user profiles. For example, we could cluster users given the number of followers or retweets. This can give a better profile of highly active users versus people tweeting rarely.

At this stage of analysis, we can use data visualization techniques to zoom out of the data and consider it in entirety. Using self-service analytics, we can look for insight not otherwise easy to see. In this example, we can use a geographical map to understand where most tweet activity is coming from. The following are some simple steps to create your geospatial view:

Step 1. In SAS Visual Analytics, add a Geo Coordinates visualization to your canvas. Note, if you have not already done so, create a geographic data element on the category that you are trying to display, in this case "User Location." This is often already provided when you have a team of data analysts providing ready to use data in SAS. If this is not done, you can easily convert any element to display on a map with drag and drop options. You can then assign data item "User Location" to the Geography role and data item "Tweet Count" to the size role with the result shown in Figure 10.3.

Figure 10.3: Geospatial analysis – data overlay on a map for much faster insight

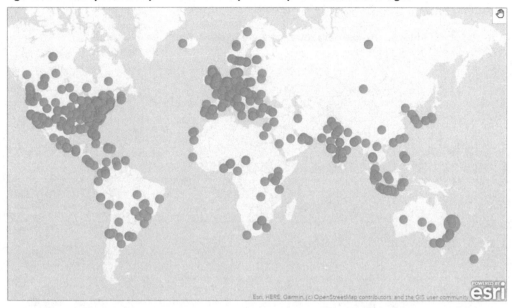

Analyzing data over a map can provide a great deal of insight fast. Data often jumps from the page when projected over a map, which allows insight into patterns, demographics, and completeness of the data set. SAS also provides quick insights of data quality when you project data on a map and includes options to instantly enrich your data from data provided by ESRI, a global geospatial software vendor, to add insight well beyond what is available in the original Twitter data. (Note: some additional costs may apply for ESRI data services.)

Step 2. Create a new page, insert a button bar control object, assign data role of "Month Name" as seen in Figure 10.4.

Figure 10.4: Data Roles pane – the data roles assigned to the button bar control

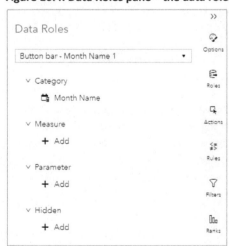

Step 3. Add a network visualization object to your report canvas, assign data roles as seen in Figure 10.5.

Figure 10.5: Data Roles pane – the data roles assigned to the network analysis object

Once completed, we can use a network visualization to see who is communicating with whom, and when they are communicating to each other. This brings your Twitter data to life and provides an interactive interface to get a feel for topology of your social network. The exploration view can be seen in Figure 10.6.

Figure 10.6: Interactive network analysis – what happens in the social network over time?

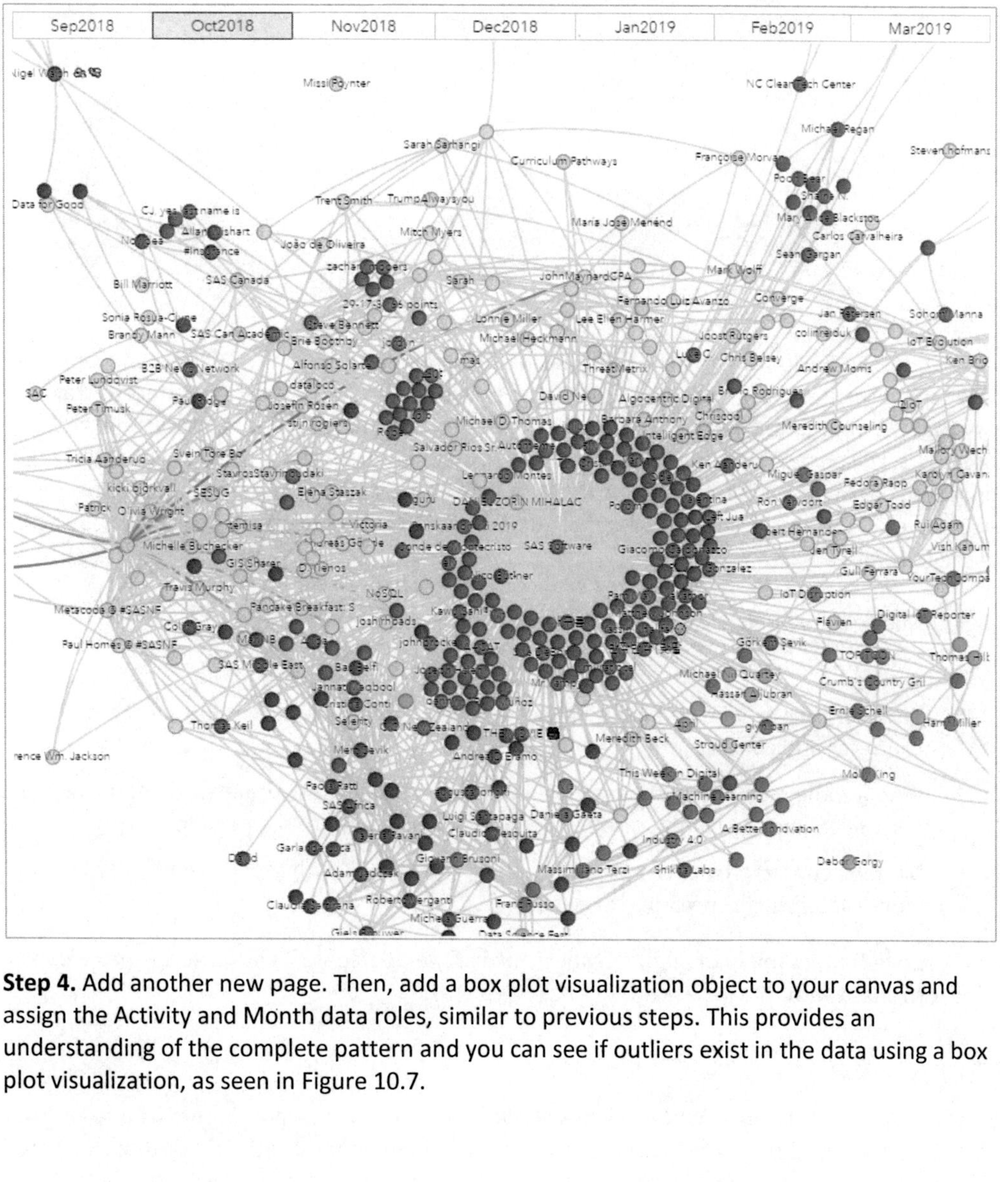

Step 4. Add another new page. Then, add a box plot visualization object to your canvas and assign the Activity and Month data roles, similar to previous steps. This provides an understanding of the complete pattern and you can see if outliers exist in the data using a box plot visualization, as seen in Figure 10.7.

Figure 10.7: Box plot – analyze outliers in the data with this useful exploration

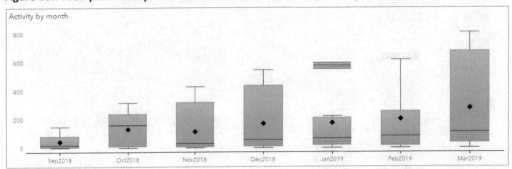

At this stage, we are looking to analyze and explore all the patterns in the Twitter data, and then see where to focus on next. Continuing with our Twitter data set, we must now start to craft the story that we want to tell our audience, as we have decided that the data is interesting, and a story exists. Of course, if this is all you wanted to achieve with this data, then you can stop at this step, save your initial exploration, and check the data as it grows over time without losing your perspective. For the purpose of this example, there are interesting facts that can be unearthed like the following:

- Number of tweets for given past period and forecast trends.

- Measure active months, weekdays, and time of day.

- Discover user profiles by analyzing location data. Do people communicate across countries and continents?

- Who are the most interesting people in the network given their network metrics? Is one person leading the communication? Who is a pulse-taker or a gatekeeper?

- Discover characteristics of people tweeting. Are people with more friends or followers more successful in spreading a message?

The list above is an example of all the richness held in the open data, like Twitter, which would be great to share with the audience.

FORMAT

Having analyzed the data and gathered insight, we can now continue our journey and tell a story. As the report author, the analyst wants to share information learned in the most impactful way. Creating impact with your analysis is often what many analysts have shared as a frustration – "Why don't the users see what this report has uncovered, and why are they using the dashboards?"

Working on many of these customer projects and trying to wow people with our outputs, we have come to understand the focus needs to be on two elements: data-driven visuals, and non-data-driven visuals.

The non-data visual elements are neglected in many data projects although they can enhance the audience experience greatly. Fonts, color, scale, real estate, and interactivity are often what lets a final dashboard down. Of course, knowing your audience is critical here because ease of use and accessibility might be the most important elements to them, and all other seemingly engaging sizzle would not benefit. These elements are explored further in this example.

Page Turner – Creating Quick Topic-Centric Landing Pages

It is important when you tell a story that you include elements like a table of contents (TOC), chapters, and headlines. If you do not take the time to create approachable entry points, then how is an audience meant to orient themselves with the story when they don't have the benefit of your time and skills with this data set? The focus areas are almost always going to match the insights that you want to share and can include the slice of the data in their headline. It is also a great idea to have a summary page or TOC for the audience to understand the key elements of your insights in one simple-to-consume location.

The following example shows three report pages, each focusing on different elements of the data.

Step 1 – As outlined earlier in this chapter, the preparation stage allows us to design a mock-up of what our pages might look like for the dashboard project and what story might be shared. This dashboard will include the following: Page 1: Location Analysis, Page 2: Relationships and Networks, and Page 3: Trend and Performance (Figure 10.8).

Figure 10.8: Mockup dashboard design – start to think with visuals early in the process

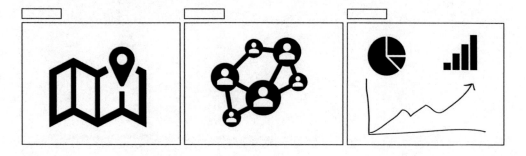

Step 2 – Building the Dashboard Pages

A general method to create the pages for this dashboard is to insert a precision container object on our page. Maximize the container to fill the entire page (property: height 100, width 100 as this represents percent). Then insert an image object into this container as a background image. This can also be set to height 100 and width 100 and can be altered to ensure the look that you need for your background. A great idea at this point is to save the container as an object for reuse in your other dashboard pages in this example.

Step 2a – Next, we use simple drag-and-drop wizards to build out our page elements for Page 1: Location Analysis. Insert a map object into the same container and add your data roles for tweet count and location. This will project your data across your map object. You can edit the map background by choosing from the standard ESRI maps included with SAS VA or use an alternate map background from your own installation of ESRI for added flexibility. If you are not interested in showing the map background, you can hide the background entirely.

Using the data from Twitter and leveraging the geospatial analysis from SAS VA, you can get a great sense of the social network by seeing the participants and where they posted from. The simple view in Figure 10.9 shows the tweet frequency across the globe for the selected data. Geospatial analysis is a very approachable projection of the data for analysts and audience because we can see the digital world overlaid onto the physical world: a map.

Figure 10.9: Page 1: Location Analysis – geospatial analysis of the tweets

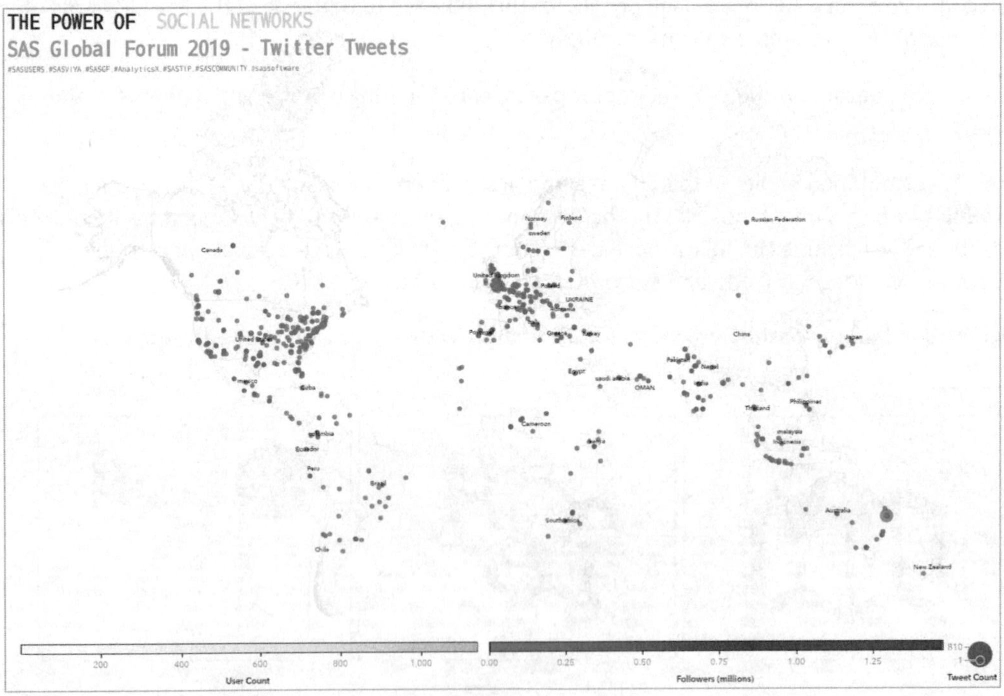

Step 2b – Page 2: Relationships and Networks. Add a new page to the dashboard and insert the previously saved container object, which included our background image to the page. Add your network analysis object and assign data roles per the exploration step, as seen in Figure 10.10.

Data visualization of complex data relationships is one of the most important features of modern software tools like SAS Visual Analytics. The interactive network visualization in Figure 10.10 is an amazing combination of visual impact of self-service exploration built into one element. Adding some additional filters and search elements to this page provides the audience with a rich self-service analysis portal, which will amaze your next team meeting with all the insight this can uncover while creating impact. Your audience will continue to come back time and again once they see how feature-rich this page is. They will, of course, be looking for themselves in the Twittersphere once they know this view is possible.

Figure 10.10: Page 2: Relationships and Networks

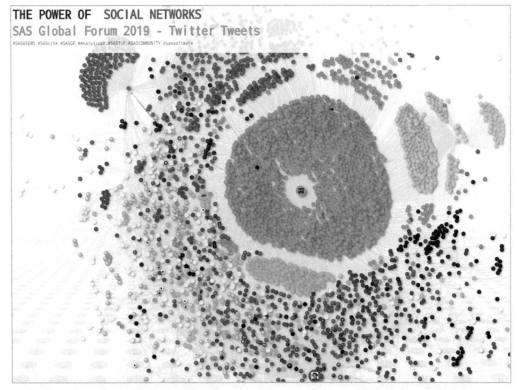

Step 2c – Page 3: Trend and Performance. Copy the last step, add a new page to the dashboard, and insert the previously saved container object that included our background image to the page. Use the precision container and add a box plot object to the page. We can now assign the data item "Edge Index" and group the analysis by Month Name. This will allow us to see the tweet frequency aggregated by month. Insert a heat map object to analyze weekday by hour and finally, use a time series to forecast tweet volume by month and add a forecast prediction to analyze what could occur in the future. A common view of data is a timeline, where you can overlay projections and performance together using the powerful time series forecasting built inside SAS Visual Analytics. Time is a very approachable view for analysis because humans are inherently in tune with timelines, and adding the ability to project and forecast allows the audience to clearly see what could happen. This view also allows some additional features for the analyst to do scenario analysis and "what if" analysis. As seen in Figure 10. 11, the analyst can provide this time view with projected values into the future, including a confidence interval for the tweet volumes: past, present and future.

Figure 10.11: Page 3: Trend and Performance

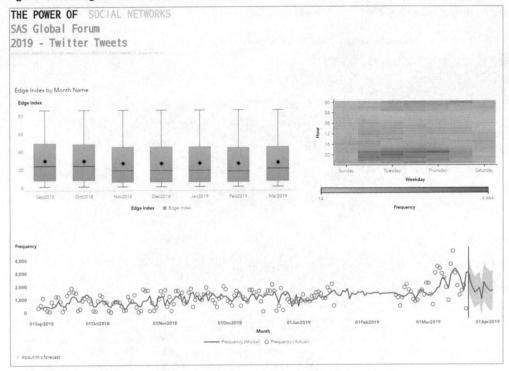

Step 3 – Add Interactivity to the Dashboard.

To make the impact that we need to keep our audience coming back to the dashboard, we want to include some guided analysis features to further focus. In this step, we look to add some interactive filters and bring the use of the dashboard to life.

Using the page-level prompts, insert "Number of Followers," which creates an automatic prompt control slider. Also insert "Relationship" from the data items, which will automatically create a button bar control. You can change these if you want and set default selections if needed, as seen in Figure 10.12.

Figure 10.12:1 Prompt controls – adding prompts using automatic prompt controls

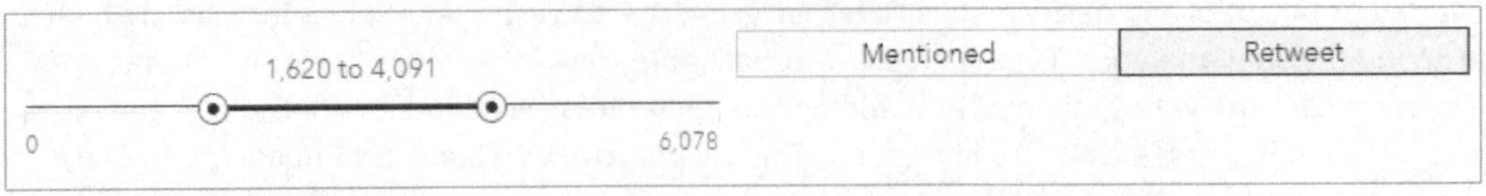

INSPIRE

REFINE

Step 4 – Test and Iterate

Run some scenarios to test the readiness of the dashboard for use by your audience. This step can include a live demonstration to key audience members – very quickly it becomes clear what is not resonating and what wows. The challenge at this stage is not agreeing to 10 more pages in this analysis because dramatic scope creep can occur. It is important to manage the expectations of the audience and ensure that you have the data to support the next iteration.

Step 5 – Share Your Dashboards

Later in the book, we look at many options to share the dashboards, and often this is simply an image in a presentation deck. Ensure that your audience can access and use the final dashboard creation for their analysis needs and be open to feedback and improvements. Always be ready to learn from the audience feedback and be agile to improve the use of the dashboard over time!

DEPLOY

How Will the Audience Access Your Dashboard?

It is important with all dashboards to consider how you will get the audience to arrive and how often they should arrive to the full-service dashboard. The dashboard elements highlighted in this example are great for sharing single infofragments from the entire dashboard as part of social media posts or embedded into websites and intranets to share some quick facts. Often, all the audience needs is a simple snippet to get on with their work, like in Figure 10.13, where the top influencer for the week can be consumed in a single bite without deviating from their daily routine. On occasion, the audience will want to dive deeper and drill through or click through to the next layer of this data journey: the dashboard. There, the analyst has created an engaging and thorough self-service application to know about the entire Twitter data set.

You can create shareable insights, which are great snack-sized entry points that you could even share back on Twitter!

Figure 10.13: Twitter infofragment – reusing the elements of the main dashboard to create a quick shareable information fragment

Creating a Poster or Infographic

Assembling your dashboard elements into a poster for display as a printed output or on a live screen for all to see is a natural next step to generate more impact from these outputs. The author is often thinking of a way to create more impact than a traditional dashboard and looks to create a large format interactive dashboard inspired by modern infographics. This provides an engaging and rich single canvas for consuming the most important information from the original dashboard. This output is also great for printing on a large format printer and making into a poster. The final output can be seen in Figure 10.14.

In Chapter 13, we look at all the ways to share these impactful entry points to the data in options like APIs, web pages, email, PowerPoint slides, and much more.

Figure 10.14: Full infographic poster – create interactive or static posters for a complete infographic

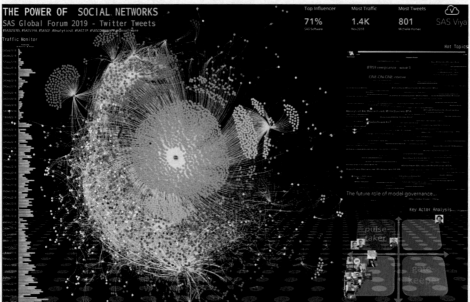

TIP: Creating the Gate-Keeper Graph

The pulse-taker and gate-keeper visualization in the bottom right of Figure 10.14 was created using a Geo Map element. In this case, the background map tiles were hidden and replaced with a static image representing the custom chart axes. Special display rules were applied to each data point using conditional Twitter profile images. The geographical coordinates were derived from SAS Viya network analytics package and related calculation of network metrics such as Betweenness and Eigenvector centrality. Both indicate a person's importance in the network graph either by representing a gate-keeper or pulse-taker. You can find out more about social network analysis at the related blog post https://blogs.sas.com/content/sascom/2014/02/19/exploring-social-networks-with-sas-visual-analytics/.

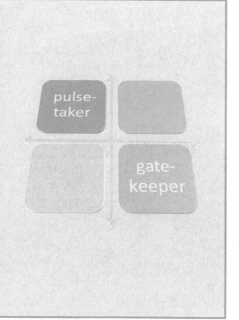

Conclusion

This social media data visualization example aimed to show how to collect data, analyze, and explore this data, and then display it as an interactive data visualization for the audience to consume the insights. Some advanced data processing techniques were leveraged in this chapter and showed how data on the internet can be analyzed for your organization to understand social media conversations using APIs and SAS. Some analytics-driven graphs were also used to show the relationships of the social network discussing SAS Global Forum. We believe that this example shows the possibilities for your own product, brand, or event data from your social media activity.

References

"Jack Dorsey." 2020. Wikipedia. Last modified August 6, 2020. https://en.wikipedia.org/wiki/Jack_Dorsey.

Christakis, Nicholas. 2010. "The hidden influence of social networks.", Filmed at TED2010 in February 2010. https://www.ted.com/talks/nicholas_christakis_the_hidden_influence_of_social_networks

Schulz, Falko. 2013. "How to import Twitter tweets in SAS DATA Step using OAuth 2 authentication style." *SAS Blogs* March 10, 2020. https://blogs.sas.com/content/sascom/2013/12/12/how-to-import-twitter-tweets-in-sas-data-step-using-oauth-2-authentication-style/ .

Schulz, Falko. 2014. "Exploring social networks with SAS Visual Analytics." *SAS Blogs: SAS Voices.* May 9, 2020. https://blogs.sas.com/content/sascom/2014/02/19/exploring-social-networks-with-sas-visual-analytics

Twitter. 2020. "Authentication." Accessed May 1, 2020.https://developer.twitter.com/en/docs/authentication/overview.

Chapter 11: Example 2: SAS and Climate Data

Overview

Example 2 is about global weather data. The topic and data set are very important to all of our lives, and the example provides some interesting insights about global temperatures over time. This example uses open data accessed from the internet and is great to show some of the core capabilities of SAS Visual Analytics and highlight approaches and techniques that you can use to reproduce this example or apply to your own data journey. In this example, we are using both the simple drag-and-drop features of SAS Visual Analytics and SAS code to show the powerful and flexible features of SAS Viya.

Audience

All SAS users can follow along with elements of this example. Some elements of this example require some advanced data wrangling skills to shape the data for final use in the dashboard design. All users will get something from this chapter because we use simple data visualization, intermediate, and advanced elements of the SAS software.

"Climate change causes and impacts are increasing rather than slowing down."

Petteri Taalas, WMO Secretary-General

Introduction

In this example, we will use Earth's surface temperatures using daily and monthly National Aeronautics and Space Administration (NASA)/GISS data for over 25,000 stations across the globe. We will go through all steps required from initial data collection, preparation, design, and building a full dashboard with many layout elements. You will be able to use the same steps in your own design projects.

According to "The Global Climate in 2015–2019," a report by the World Meteorological Organization (WMO), the five-year period of 2015–2019 has been the worst in terms of global warming and resultant climate change impacts (WMO 2019). The goal of this data visualization project is to analyze changes in Earth's surface temperatures compared to pre- and postindustrial times. Climate change – such as sea level rise, ice loss, and extreme weather continues to increase. Analyzing historic trends and weather patterns is important for everyone in order to measure the impact humans have on planet Earth.

INFORM

ACCESS

Getting access to the data can often be challenging. This challenge is related to the legal permissions required to use the data or simply having data that is not in the right format or structure that you require. For this example, we used open data from NASA and National Oceanic and Atmospheric Administration (NOAA) that was published on global historical temperature data as part of the Global Historical Climatology Network (GHCN). We also included results of the related GISS Surface Temperature Analysis (GISTEMP v4) for hundreds of weather stations around the world. GHCN data is provided in text files and fixed-column layout (GHCN 2019). Since the data was provided in such special format, we decided to use the custom code developed in SAS Studio in order to import the data into SAS Viya (Figure 11.1).

Figure 11.1: SAS Studio Code Editor

GISTEMP is provided as compressed Network Common Data Form (netCDF) files (.NC file extension, regular 2°×2° grid), and the import into SAS requires a conversion to comma-separated value (CSV) file first. We converted the NC files to CSV files using the open-source Climate Data Operators (CDO) tool (https://code.mpimet.mpg.de/projects/cdo). The following command was used for the conversion:

```
cdo outputtab,date,lon,lat,value gistemp1200_GHCNv4_ERSSTv5.nc >
gistemp1200_GHCNv4_ERSSTv5.csv
```

The resulting CSV file (which is tab-delimited) can be directly imported into SAS Viya for processing. See the sample files for the full SAS code snippet used here.

EXPLORE

Before starting with the actual design of our infographics, let's explore the data and discover interesting insights worthy of sharing in the final report. During the exploration, you can validate data quality, discover potential issues, or simply learn about suitable ways of representing information using the best possible visualization.

The data provided is all about historical surface temperature changes across the globe. Some of the questions that we are trying to answer include the following:

- Have there been any temperature changes over the years at all?
- How do temperature anomalies compare to the base reference period 1950–1980?
- Are changes the same across the globe? Are some latitude zones or pole regions affected more than others?
- Do monthly mean global surface temperatures increase or decrease?
- Does the Northern or Southern Hemisphere show the same result?
- Do some years show an exceptional difference compared to others?
- How do seasons (for example, winter and summer) compare across years?
- Are there any hotspots across the globe with higher than average readings?
- Given the 25K+ stations in the inventory, do they all provide the same year coverage?

To answer some of these questions and to gain further understanding of the data, let's dive into SAS Visual Analytics and load the previously imported data. Note that the global mean temperature anomalies shown in the graphics below are always based on the reference years 1950–1980. We are starting with the GHCN weather station data (*GHCND_STATIONS* table) to first get a feel where the temperature sensor data is coming from. A great visualization to use at this stage is a geographical map. Figure 11.2 shows the distribution of weather stations globally and in the United States. Conveniently, station information includes related map coordinates along with station name and elevation. Refer to this book's example code and data for advanced data preparation.

Figure 11.2: Weather station geographical distribution

Coloring by the number of years of each station's data shows the distribution of areas with the longest service. Before looking into individual station or region data, let's have a look at some global measures using the *GISTEMP_MONTHLY_ANOMALY* table that contains monthly global means. A simple time series line plot by year is shown in Figure 11.3.

Figure 11.3: Global mean surface temperatures compared to 1950–1980 average

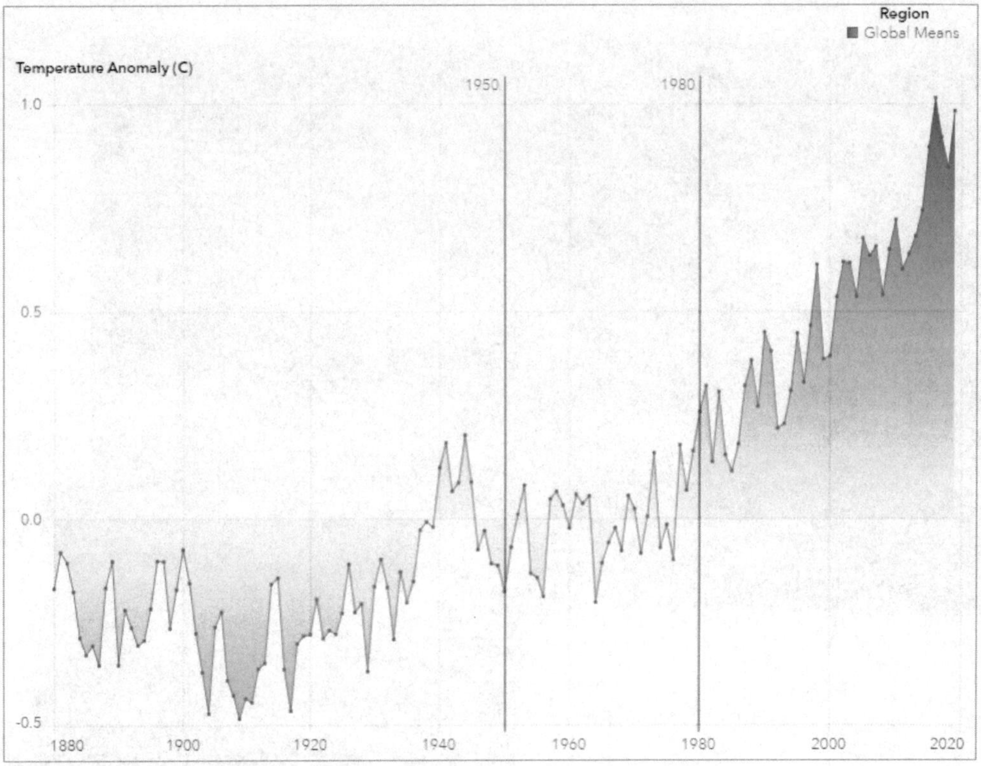

We can see that overall temperatures increased (a positive anomaly value) compared to the reference years 1950–1980 with especially high readings in recent years. The year 2016 was one of the hottest on record. Do temperature increases occur evenly across the globe? Find out by comparing the Northern and Southern Hemispheres as shown in Figure 11.4.

Figure 11.4: Hemispheric means compared to 1950-1980 average

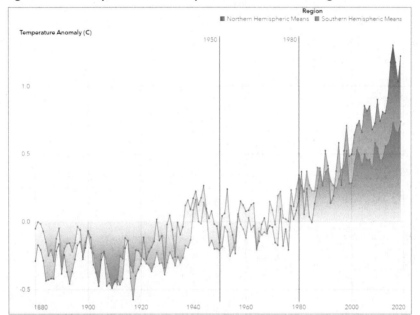

It seems that the Northern Hemisphere shows higher than average readings compared to the base reference years. This could be something to explore further when comparing latitude zone or polar region data. The data also provides information on a month level and as such, we can compare seasonal cycles over the years. The following chart shows the monthly global means by 20-year intervals.

Figure 11.5: Seasonal cycles since 1980

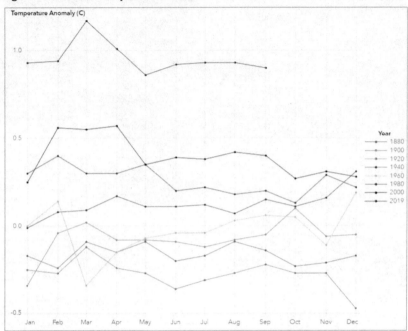

The visualization again confirms higher readings in recent years. It also shows a trend that we typically see higher anomalies beginning the year – likely caused by the overall higher values for the Northern Hemisphere and related warmer winter seasons.

INSIGHT

ANALYZE

Now, let's look at the gridded surface air temperatures anomaly data provided by the netCDF files imported earlier. The following contour plot on a geographical map shows the global means for the year 2018.

Figure 11.6: Gridded surface air temperature anomaly (2018)

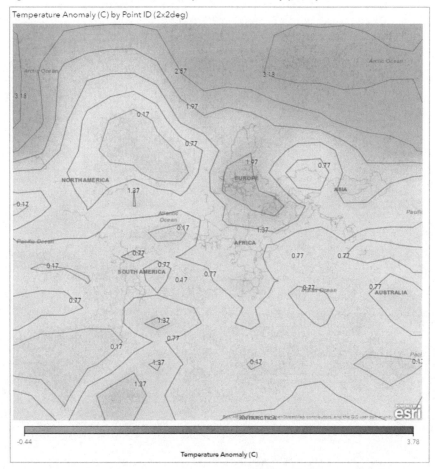

We can see hotspots of higher than average temperature changes especially in the Northern Hemisphere near Europe and the polar regions, which is expected given the results of previous visualizations.

Grouping data into latitude zones also confirms this observation, as shown in Figure 11.7.

Figure 11.7: Temperature anomaly at the poles

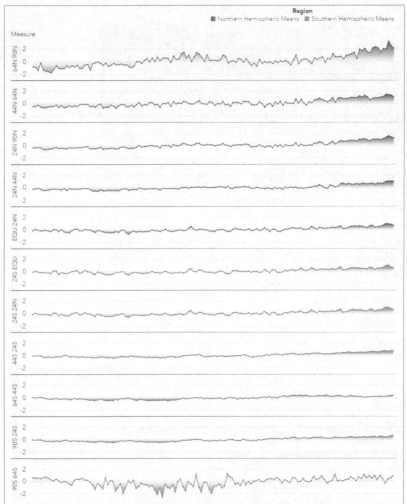

While we could dive into the actual data analysis further and apply things like advanced analytics, this example focuses on the design and reporting aspects on the data that we have wrangled. We have collected enough information to understand the data structure, quality, and high-level trends.

FORMAT

Having analyzed the data and gathered insight, we can now continue our journey and tell a story. As the analyst, we want to share information learned in the most impactful way. Initial page design mock-ups should reflect our audience who could either be data scientists trying to understand details about our analysis or even the general public, given the increased interest and political coverage in recent years.

For the purpose of this example, the analyst decided to describe the steps required for a basic infographic dashboard covering information about global temperature changes on monthly and yearly levels. While you could start designing your graphics layout in the tool itself, it is often easier to use a whiteboard or tools like PowerPoint for the initial mock-up design. This way, you don't get distracted by tool features and avoid being forced into a specific design structure. Figure 11.8 shows the rough initial design using a whiteboard mockup.

Figure 11.8: Initial design

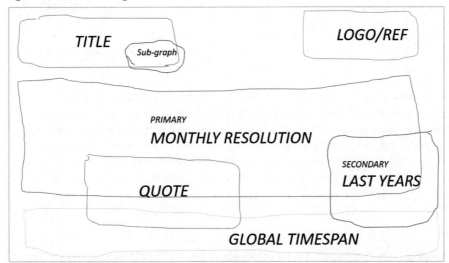

The idea is to have a primary (line) graph that shows the most recent years of monthly global temperature changes in the center and support it by a secondary (bar) chart to the right showing the yearly resolution.

We are planning to add a third (bar) graph at the bottom showing the entire history of data available, starting with the year 1788. To give the report a more infographic appeal, we are also going to add a bold title along with a supporting quote. While this is a relatively simple infographic, we will be able to cover a few basic design skills during creation. We are envisioning a darker color palette for the entire infographic, so we will use very dark gray background (color hex code #343433) with mostly white foreground text.

The next step in the design process is to lay out the proposed objects in SAS Visual Analytics. As the design requires overlaying objects on top of each other, the first step is to add a special container type supporting it.

TIP: The Precision Container

The Precision container behaves just like a PowerPoint slide and enables you to lay out objects freely on a grid. You can hold the CTRL key down during drag, and an even finer grid will enable you to position objects more accurately. You can also control object sizes within the container either by drag and drop or by adjusting size and position in the Objects pane.

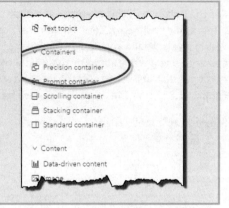

We are also going to adjust the report size to a fixed pixel ratio (1300x980px). This enables us to design the graphics regardless of final screen resolution and ensures that objects are always sized and aligned according to our settings. While you could also use the default responsive layout, some object components (for example, text) do not scale as well as graph objects and might cause unexpected scroll bars or rendering. You can set a fixed report size in the Options pane using the report-level options. It is important to understand and test the render on mobile or desktop when setting absolute sizing.

BUILD

Let's add the proposed graph objects into our container and build the actual report page. You could either use the ready-to-use page templates or start with a blank canvas in SAS Visual Analytics. None of the templates seem to fit in this case, so we are going to drag and drop objects into the precision container and align them per our initial design. Figure 11.9 shows the graphs rendered as expected based on the sample data.

Figure 11.9: Initial design in SAS Visual Analytics

While building your report, it is important to keep track of the objects that you have added. An excellent tool is the Outline pane. It shows the hierarchical structure of a report, providing access to object-specific actions. The Outline pane enables you to interact with objects even though you might not be able to see them on the canvas (for example, one object might be overlaid by another object). Using the right-click menu provides access to object options. For better reference, you might consider renaming objects to better reflect what they represent as shown in Figure 11.10.

Figure 11.10: Default and customized object names

Now let's bring the graphics to life by adding the *GHCNM_STATION_DATA_AWS* data source. This table contains the aggregated monthly temperature (in degrees Celsius) and temperature changes (compared to the base period) since data recording started. Let's start with the bottom bar chart, which should visualize the temperature changes since 1788. Given that the chart will show data on year level, we are going to create a copy of the *Date* variable by right-clicking and selecting Duplicate, and then selecting the *Year* format. Assigning this newly created variable *Year* to the bar chart as shown in Figure 11.11 provides a first sobering look of the visual.

Figure 11.11: Unformatted data from the GHCNM_STATION_DATA_AWS table

To achieve the desired rendering, we are going to apply the following option changes:

- Sort date ascending by year
- Change the aggregation for variable *Temperature Anomaly (C)* to average
- Remove the graph grid lines
- Remove the X- and Y-axis labels, lines, and tick values
- Add two text objects to the left and the right of the graph showing the start and end years
- Add display rules to color code the bars given their temperature anomaly. We used the following color codes and rules, as shown in Figure 11.1:
  - value > 1: #C8346F
  - 0.5 < value < 1: #B23196
  - 0 < value < 0.5: #7B3DBA
  - -0.5 < value < 0: #5839B5
  - -1 value < -0.5: #425CBC
  - value < -1: #2AAFE0

Figure 11.12: Display Rules

Figure 11.13 shows the resulting visual. The additional coloring of bars gives a much better visual support for higher and lower temperature changes over the years.

Figure 11.13: Resulting visual with color and additional options

Let's investigate the primary center graph now. This visualization shows the seasonal variations of temperature changes. Using a line chart here would be great due to the nature of time series data. Now, like before, we are creating a copy of the *Date* variable and specifying the *Month* format. Adding this newly created variable and group by *Year* to the center chart shows a rather cluttered first glance of the data (Figure 11.14).

Figure 11.14: The primary center graph before revisions

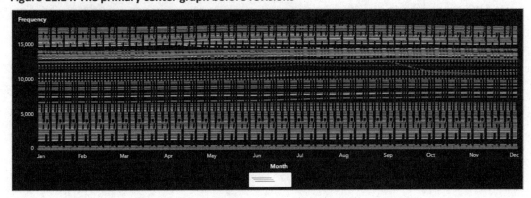

Given the high number of years, we are going to reduce data for rendering and showcase the last 20 years. However, even 20 years is a relatively high number of lines to be rendering on top of each other. We are using additional display rules to highlight only the last 8 years. We are going to apply the following changes to the graph:

- Add a filter for Year >= 2012
- Remove the graph grid lines
- Turn on markers (size = 3)
- Change the line thickness to 2
- Show the data labels (text style 12, bold)
- X-axis options
  - Remove the axis label
- Y-axis options
  - Remove the axis label
  - Set a fixed minimum = -1
  - Set a fixed maximum = 3
  - Add a reference line at 0.94 (label = "20th Century Average")
- Line/Marker colors:
  - 2012: #97368E
  - 2013: #5839B5
  - 2014: #6538AC
  - 2015: #E03361
  - 2016: #DD5757
  - 2017: #C13473
  - 2018: #97368E
  - 2019: #81379B
- Turn the legend visibility off

Figure 11.15 shows the rendered graph with all changes above applied.

Figure 11.15: Monthly temperature changes from 2012–2019

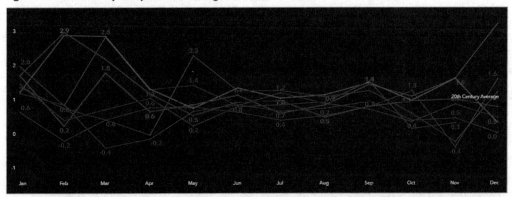

Additionally, we want to highlight the fact that we have many more years of data, so we are going to add back the previous filtered-out 12 years. Now, for better visualization and not taking the focus away from the main graph, we want those years to fade into the background and barely be visible. To achieve that effect, we are creating a copy of the above graph (right-click, and select Duplicate) and making the following changes:

- Change all the Line/Marker colors to a dark gray color (hex color 3D4550)
- Reduce line thickness to 1
- Remove all data labels
- Change the layout position and the size to be exactly on top of the original graph
- Move the new graph to the back so that the original graph overlays on top
- Remove the X- and Y-axis labels and the tick values

The result is a nicely faded graph behind the primary visualization (Figure 11.16).

Figure 11.16: Monthly temperature changes with a background graph

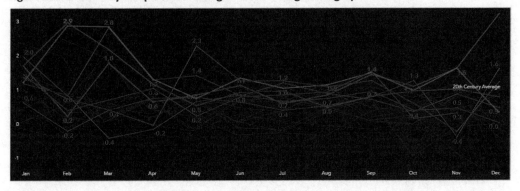

Lastly, let's work on the overlaying the bar chart to the right of the initial design. As you have noticed, we removed the legend in one of the previous steps when modifying the line chart properties. Every graph needs a legend if the colors or the symbols are not self-explanatory. We removed the original legend because we wanted to replace it with a richer bar chart that shows the yearly aggregated values. Special care is required here to synchronize the colors between the line and the bar chart.

The bar chart uses the previously created *Year* variable as category and the temperature change as the bar height. As before, the initial rendering in Figure 11.17 isn't too appealing at first.

Figure 11.17: Initial bar chart rendering

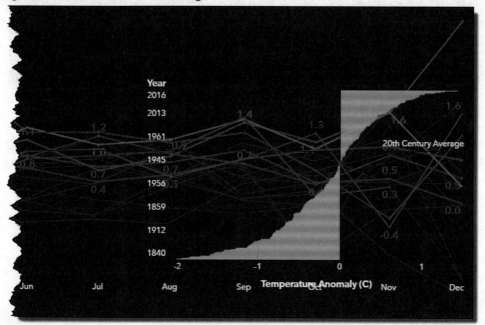

To improve the rendering, we are going to apply the following options:

- Add a filter for Year >= 2012
- Remove the object title
- Reduce the object size to 15% width and 25% height and align to the right
- Remove graph grid lines
- Add segment labels (text size 10)
- Y-Axis options
  - Remove labels
  - Remove line

- X-Axis options
    - Remove labels
    - Remove line
    - Remove tick values
- Line/Marker colors:
    - 2012: 97368E
    - 2013: 5839B5
    - 2014: 6538AC
    - 2015: E03361
    - 2016: DD5757
    - 2017: C13473
    - 2018: 97368E
    - 2019: 81379B
- Increase the transparency to 20%

The above changes help readers to identify years with high versus low temperature changes in Figure 11.18.

Figure 11.18: The last eight years of temperature changes

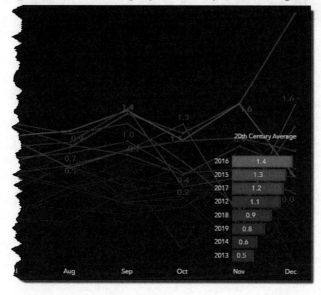

INSPIRE

REFINE

The final tweaks include adding the top left banner, as well as adding the SAS Viya logo along with some additional text about the data sources that are used. We used PowerPoint to create the faded background banner image that includes the "tipping point" graphic. If you don't need a fancy banner, you might want to use the built-in text objects that allow rich text formatting.

To further support the rising temperature changes and tipping of the related graphics, we overlaid the banner image with an additional line chart that shows temperature changes by year. While this is optional, it gives it a nice supporting touch.

Figure 11.19: The banner for the report

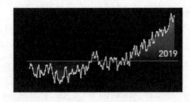 

The final version of the infographic also includes a quotation to further support the message about rising temperatures globally. Note that we used a custom image for the double quotation marks, which nicely visualizes the text as a quote. You can also use the text object here with special formatting. The final infographic renders as shown in Figure 11.20.

Figure 11.20: The final infographic

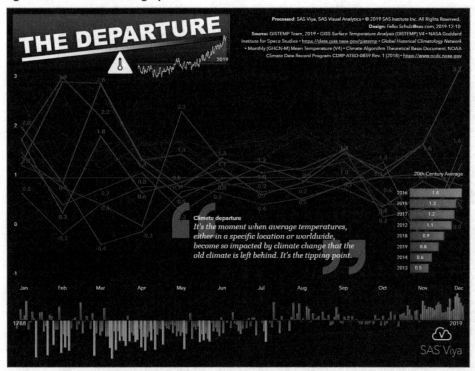

To view a video compilation of this infographic segment and see how the design process is done in the application, go to https://youtu.be/RiFoAH-XWiY.

DEPLOY

Taking this a step further, the analyst also decided to include the preceding segment into an even larger graphic covering all aspects of surface air temperature data and related analysis (bottom left of Figure 11.21). The infographic shows the distribution of weather stations globally and their years of service. The viewer will also learn about temperature anomalies at the poles and general impact of changes around the world.

Breaking down complex infographics into smaller dashboards is a common practice and makes the development and design process easier. It also helps to structure such large-scale posters into segments and topic of interest. In this example, different background gradients help consumers to differentiate between analysis results of weather stations, as well as seasonal and global air temperature measurements.

Figure 11.21: The full-size infographic poster

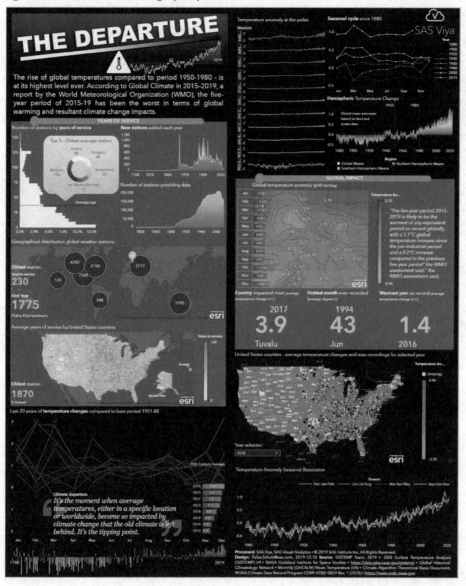

Conclusion

Open data holds the key to understanding climate change and the risks to humankind. This example provided a quick overview of how you can access and analyze the data about global climate over many years. This data can be visualized in many ways, including time and geography, which can be great to provide fast insight for your audience. The data journey that we created here could be delivered in many formats like a dashboard, an infographic poster, or as series of smaller slices to share via social media. We encourage you to load this data and share your own insights and visualizations via the SAS Communities website. Together we can make a difference by showing climate data in new ways.

References

GISTEMP Team. 2019. GISS Surface Temperature Analysis (GISTEMP), version 4. NASA Goddard Institute for Space Studies. Data set accessed November 21, 2019. https://data.giss.nasa.gov/gistemp

Lenssen, Nathan J.L., Gavin A. Schmidt, James E. Hansen, Matthew J. Menne, Avraham Persin, Reto-Ruedy, and Daniel Zyss. 2019. Improvements in the GISTEMP uncertainty model. Journal of Geophysical Research: Atmospheres, 124, no. 12, 6307-6326, doi:10.1029/2018JD029522

NOAA. 2019. Global Historical Climatology Network - Monthly (GHCN-M) Mean Temperature (Version 4) - Climate Algorithm Theoretical Basis Document, NOAA Climate Data Record Program CDRP-ATBD-0859 Rev. 1. 2018. Data set accessed November 21, 2019. https://www.ncdc.noaa.gov/data-access/land-based-station-data/land-based-datasets/global-historical-climatology-network-monthly-version-4

Schulz, Falko. 2020. "Best Practices for Effective Infographics in SAS® Visual Analytics." In Proceedings of the SAS® Global Forum 2020 Conference. Cary, NC: SAS Institute Inc.. https://www.sas.com/content/dam/SAS/support/en/sas-global-forum-proceedings/2020/4126-2020.pdf

World Meteorological Organization. 2019. "Global Climate in 2015–2019: Climate change accelerates." 23 September 2019. https://public.wmo.int/en/media/press-release/global-climate-2015-2019-climate-change-accelerates

Chapter 12: Example 3: SAS and Outbreak Data

Overview

Data visualization and analytical models have been thrust into each of our lives. The global pandemic of the Coronavirus Disease 2019 (COVID-19) has highlighted the importance of data and dashboards for providing facts to the global population. This example does not step through scientific approaches on health data. We leave that to the epidemiologists. This chapter steps through approaching open global health data and how we can access, explore, and visualize to provide self-service dashboards for others to use. This example is based on some initial work that led to the SAS global COVID-19 dashboard, which was provided during the pandemic for everyone to use for their own analysis on their country and other countries around the world.

Audience

All SAS users will be able to take ideas from this example as we leverage simple drag-and-drop tools, and also look at some data challenges that came up over time. Novice, intermediate, and advanced SAS users will all learn features from this global health data example using SAS Visual Analytics on SAS Viya.

> *"Whenever I am infuriated, I revenge myself with a new diagram."*

> *Florence Nightingale*

Introduction

The global COVID-19 pandemic confirmed to all people in the world the importance of data in the response to global health issues. This example will use open data sources from across the world and combine them to create a comprehensive and flexible dashboard for the audience. Health data is one of the main open data challenges the world faces. With accurate and consistent data, the global community can act as one in response to outbreaks like COVID-19. These techniques can be applied to other demographic and open data sources as we look to analyze populations and cases over time.

INFORM

ACCESS

As with every data visualization project, we need to get access to data supporting our data visualization requirements. Given that this pandemic is a global issue, there have been many various data sources available across the globe. Many provide data in unstructured format only – others such as John Hopkins University CSSE (JHU), European Center of Disease Control (ECDC), or even news agencies such as the New York Times share data via text files on GitHub. Due to the complex data structure and variety of sources, SAS decided to publish ready-to-use import scripts on https://github.com/sassoftware/covid-19-sas to read COVID-19 data into SAS Viya for data visualization purposes.

The data that we are going to analyze contain information about confirmed cases of novel coronavirus infections by country since recording began in 2020. Many countries also provide the total number of deaths or recoveries.

Importing the data is just a matter of executing the script provided in SAS Studio (Figure 12.1).

Figure 12.1: SAS Studio import script execution

EXPLORE

Data imported not only provides information about confirmed cases, recovered, and deaths, but also provides accumulated statistics such as double rates. The script takes care of correct data mapping for geographical regions, and we can go straight into data visualization to explore the data.

To get a first glimpse of the virus spread, we are going to configure a geographical item by using the COUNTRY data item and specify the "Country or Region Names" as a suitable lookup mechanism. Visualizing the "Confirmed" cases by COUNTRY using a regional map shows the output in Figure 12.2.

Figure 12.2: Confirmed cases by country (data shown as of May 2020)

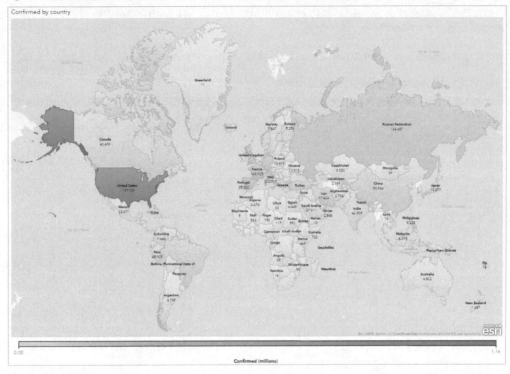

The data provides insights in cases over time, and we have information available on a daily basis. To get an understanding on the time period available, let's visualize the total number of cases over time for a few selected countries using a time series plot as shown in Figure 12.3.

Figure 12.3: Total confirmed cases over time

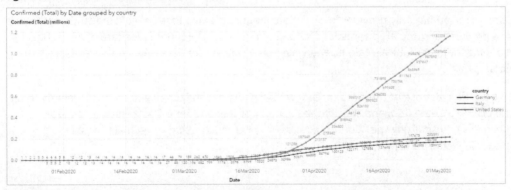

Interestingly, but not surprising, many countries had cases very early in the outbreak but were reluctant to start actions until the outbreak was well underway. Note that prior to March in Figure 12.3, all countries had less than 100 cases. As with every outbreak, quick decisions on how to prevent further spreading (for example, a city lockdown) decided how the curve and related double rates would develop.

Later in the analysis, we will also use a different X-time-axis as a common base for comparison. Because the outbreak started on different dates in each country, it will be easier to compare curves if we create a new date field that represents the number of days since 1st, 10th, or 100th case. While just a numeric number, it will be easier to compare related double and growth rates.

INSIGHT

ANALYZE

To fully understand the outbreak and impact, we not only need to compare actual case or death numbers but also investigate incidence and prevalence measures. While there are different models to calculate such numbers for the purpose of this book, we are going to use the following:

- Incidence: New confirmed cases / country population
- Prevalence: Total confirmed cases / country population

In both cases, we are taking the total population of a country into account. Related data is freely available from sources such as United Nations (2020) or World Bank indicators (2020). SAS Visual Analytics provides the ability to create calculated items via dragging and dropping them, so we are going to create a new item named "Incidence (/100k)" as shown in Figure 12.4.

Figure 12.4: Incidence calculated item

Given this calculation, we can now plot data using a time or numeric series graph in SAS Visual Analytics. Figure 12.5 shows the graph plotted using the actual date the cases were recorded – whereas Figure 12.6 shows the same graph but using the number of days since 100th new cases. The latter allows a much better curve comparison since all data points have a common start point.

Figure 12.5: Incidence rate by population and date period

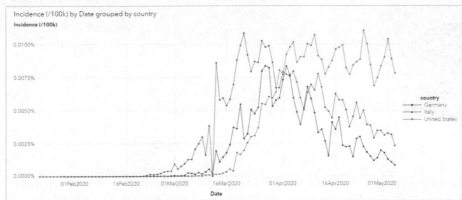

Figure 12.6: Incidence rate by population since 100th case

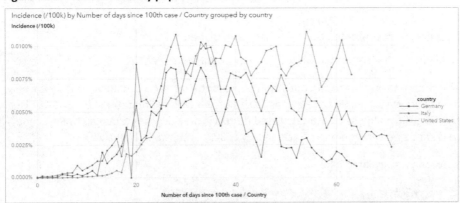

You can now clearly see that countries such as Italy have fought against this outbreak for a much longer time than others. However, each country shares a similar exponential curve at the beginning of the outbreak – though resulting in different case development as time goes on, dependent on preventive measures being implement on country level.

Another measure that is often used in measuring new cases growth is the "doubling rate" or "days to double," which is a relatively simple measure telling you how many days it took for a number to double. The script provided already performs this calculation for us so that we can visualize it using a bar-line chart – allowing us to compare both the actual total number of cases and growth. Figure 12.7 shows an example for the selected country "United States." Note, that we are also using the number of days since 100th case as the common X axis.

Figure 12.7: Days to double for country United States

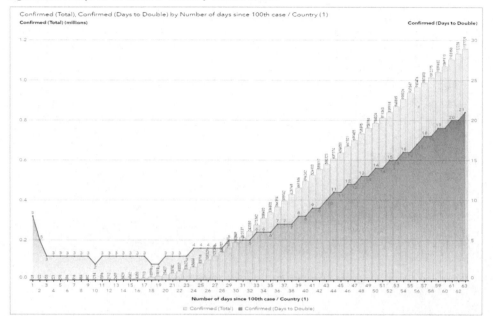

A final analysis involves looking at case fatality rates (CFR). This relatively simple measure (total deaths divided by total confirmed cases) allows a better comparison between countries because we are not just looking at total numbers. Building this type of calculated measure in SAS Visual Analytics is quickly done using the built-in calculated item editor as shown in Figure 12.8.

Figure 12.8: Formula to calculate CFR

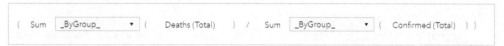

For validation, we are plotting this measure against the total confirmed cases using a dual-time series graph (Figure 12.9).

Figure 12.9: Comparing CFR with confirmed cases

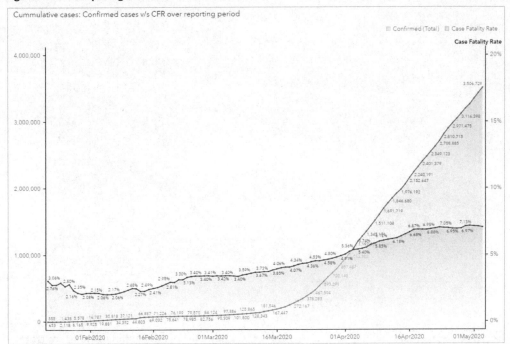

The visualization confirms the expected increase in CFR with increasing number of cases and deaths. Later in our final dashboard, we can offer a country-based comparison or selection for more detailed analysis.

FORMAT

In order to compile all information into a single dashboard, we are going to split the dashboard into three separate pages – each covering a different aspect of this global virus outbreak (Table 12.10).

Table 12.10: Report structure

Global Status	Location Analysis	Trend Analysis
Global geographical map view comparing total new cases	Statistics for a single selected country	Curve comparison for selected countries
Last week's numbers and top impacted countries by number of new daily cases	Provide details on province/state level based on new cases and deaths	Total number of cases by number of days since 1st, 10th, and 100th case
Top 10 countries based on total number of cases and deaths	Total cases over time	Time series plot visualizing days to double
	Geographical map showing state level information	

In order to design this dashboard, we are going to create a new report and create a new "template" page first. The reason for such page is the idea to reuse this page as template for other pages. Given that we want to create at least three pages as per Table 12.10, we don't want to create things like banners or footers on every page. A common technique is to create a template page first.

Template

A template page is created quickly. For this example, we are going to apply a simple page structure with a banner, main content section, and footer. We are going to add common icons and brand images along with some useful information such as last updated date. The Outline pane shows the following structure for our page (Figure 12.11).

Figure 12.11: Template page structure

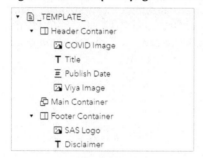

The "Main Container" can either be a standard flow container or precision container, depending on how visualizations need to be positioned. Both the header and the footer container have a fixed height specified (10%). The template page created in SAS Visual Analytics will look like Figure 12.12.

Figure 12.12: Sample template page

We are also going to hide this page so that it can be permanently part of our report without appearing in the final rendering. This way, we can continue to use this template for future additions to the report.

Page 1: Global Status

In order to create our first report, we are now going to duplicate the previously created template page. After unhiding the page (remember our template page was hidden) and specifying its new name "Global Status," the page is ready for use.

As outlined before, the purpose of this page is to cover details on global level, so we are going to start off with a geographical view of all countries with known cases. We previously created the country geographical data item, so we are simply going to add a geo regional map and assign country data item along with confirmed cases. Regional geographical maps also allow us to embed data labels and values, which nicely enhances the map visualization. Given this is a global outbreak and almost every country on earth is affected, the country boundaries represented an almost complete picture of Earth. This means that for simplicity, we can also hide the actual map background. A first glimpse on such map rendering is shown in Figure 12.13.

Figure 12.13: Confirmed cases by country map view

Let's also include details about the last week's confirmed cases. Rather than just using a single bar with total numbers, we are going to stack the top five impacted countries. This will visualize countries being impacted most over the last seven days (Figure 12.14).

Figure 12.14: Top five impacted countries over last seven days

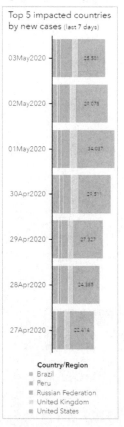

Creating a stacked bar is not difficult. It is just a matter of assigning a group variable (Country in this case). However, we cannot just simply add to top K-ranks here in order to show the last seven days as well as top five impacted countries. Ranks in SAS Visual Analytics are both applied on the detail level data, and given that we want the top five countries impacted on a specific day (versus all data), this would result in a wrong list order. Therefore, we are going to use a single rank and a filter instead. First, we add a rank for the "top 5 count" based on the total confirmed cases number and then we use a filter to only show the last seven days. The filter expression used is shown in Figure 12.15.

Figure 12.15: Filter the last seven days

Finally, we are also going to add a simple list of top 10 countries and their related figures for confirmed cases, deaths, and prevalence. To make the list table easier to read and compare numbers, we are also going to add colored cell bars (Figure 12.16).

Figure 12.16: Top 10 countries by confirmed cases and deaths

Outbreak by country (Top 10)

Country/ Region	Total Confirmed Cases ▾	Prevalence (/100k)	Deaths (Total)
United States	1.2M	354	
Spain	217K	465	
Italy	211K	349	
United Kingdom	188K	283	
France	169K	252	
Germany	166K	200	
Russian Federation	135K	93	
Turkey	126K	153	
Iran	97K	119	
China	84K	6	
All Other	956K	12,191	

Merging all visualization into a single page design along with some additional key values represents our global status page as shown in Figure 12.17.

Figure 12.17: Page 1: Global Status

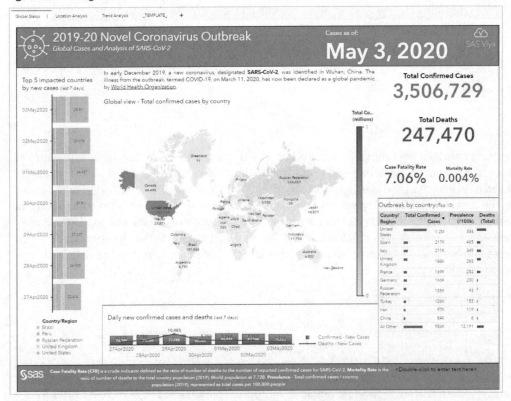

Page 2: Location Analysis

The location analysis page is where interested viewers can dive into more details for a particular region. Many countries provide more granular outbreak data given their local geographical administrative levels. Data for the United States, for instance, is provided on both the state and county level.

This page will have a basic structure but will allow the user to select or enter the desired country using a control object. These objects can be linked to other visualizations and apply related detail data filtering. The following example shows the control with selected county United States and key values representing the country's data (Figure 12.18).

Figure 12.18: Infographic widget showing country key stats

We are also going to provide a list and geographical view of state/province information. Using a similar design for the list table (same header, same colored cell bars) will provide consistent rendering throughout the report similar to the geographical map, which will have the same color theme (Figure 12.19).

Figure 12.19: State/Province-level visualizations

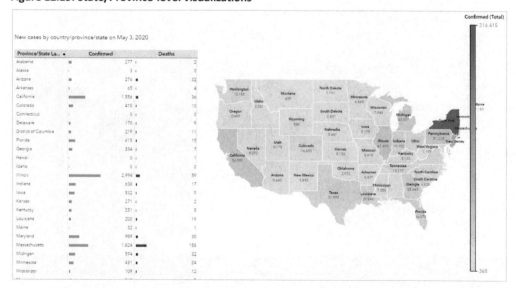

Lastly, we are going to add a detailed description of the country's current state using a text object. This object will describe (in words), given today's data, how many cases and deaths have occurred along with predicted growth rate using the days to double measure. SAS Visual

Analytics allows us to assign data items to a text object, which are then available as variables in the text editor (Figure 12.20).

Figure 12.20: Text object with data items

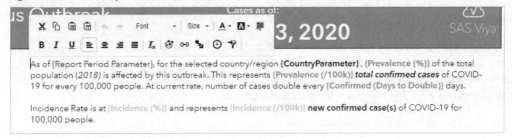

Merging all visualizations together in single design shows our location analysis page as follows (Figure 12.21).

Figure 12.21: Page 2: Location Analysis

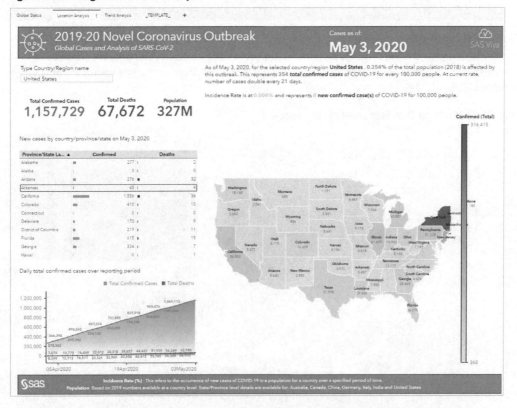

Page 3: Trend Analysis

The trend analysis page covers all visualizations related to historic and predicted analysis (Figure 12.22). Users can explore this part of the dashboard to discover the development of cases over time and use measures such as days to double to detect growth.

Given the number of visuals to be added here, we are going to use a stack container and show only one visual along with controls in one container. This will allow enough real estate for the visual to render any fine details.

Given the focus on design and overall dashboard development, we are not going into much detail on each single visual. All of the sections use the same layout with a country-based control to the left (allowing the selection of one or more countries to compare) and the main series plot to the right. The following example shows Section 1 with the confirmed cases curve shown for five countries. Similar to previous examples, we are using again the number of days since 100th case as the base comparison axis.

Figure 12.22: Page 3: Trend Analysis

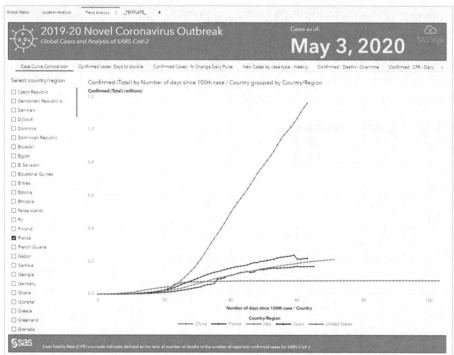

INSPIRE

REFINE

Further improvement of the dashboard should include alignment of data visualizations to provide a common layout across all pages. If possible, all pages should provide the same look and feel and allow users to find what they are looking for quickly. For instance, page controls or other filter items should be placed at the same location.

We can also consider providing more interactive visualizations to better represent the outbreak of the virus. Often, graph animations are useful here. Given that we have data on date and country, an animation could be used to show the spread of the virus over time. SAS Visual Analytics supports animations via a dedicated "animation" role available in the roles panel as shown in Figure 12.23. Dependent on the granularity of your date item, animation can be on any time level (for example, by day, by hour, and so on).

Figure 12.23: Roles panel with animation role

Once the animation role is assigned, an animation bar will appear below the visualization allowing either for automatic play of the animation or for a manual step through of each date period (Figure 12.24).

Figure 12.24: Animation bar control

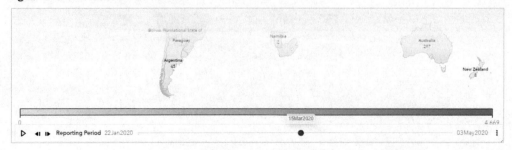

Finally, we are going to include additional help and references in the footer section. Information includes time stamps for last updated data and any explanation needed to understand some of the applied measures (for example, define "case fatality rate" for users). Depending on the amount of additional information needed, you can also consider using dedicated help pages that can be shown as "info window" dialog boxes. Such pages can be linked from other visualizations or even simple "help" icons.

DEPLOY

A dashboard can be deployed in many ways. The most common and simplest way is to share the related link to the live dashboard with your users. SAS Visual Analytics provides an option in the report menu to copy a unique link (Figure 12.25). You can also consider using the "guest access" option that allows users without an active account to view the dashboard content.

Figure 12.25: Copy link dialog box

A great alternative way to share results is to use the SAS Visual Analytics SDK, which is a software development kit. The SAS Visual Analytics SDK is a collection of JavaScript libraries that web developers can use to embed SAS Visual Analytics content within custom web pages and web apps. The SAS Visual Analytics SDK provides a framework that enables you to perform the following tasks:

- Embed entire reports or individual charts and objects from SAS Visual Analytics reports
- Embed charts and objects from multiple SAS Visual Analytics reports
- Support actions between SAS Visual Analytics report objects on your web page or in your web app
- Share data between SAS Visual Analytics report objects on your web page or in your web app

The ability to embed report sections or visualizations is especially useful for creating customized landing pages for users to start navigating a dashboard. The combination of standard HTML text and images with special SAS Visual Analytics visualizations provides a rich experience for the audience. A good example of such a landing page at the time of writing is the COVID-19 tracking page from SAS that is shown in Figure 12.26. The page combines textual information as well as visualizations such as key value or geographical objects in a single page.

Figure 12.26: SAS COVID-19 tracking page using VA SDK

Conclusion

COVID-19 data sets may be the most viewed in history, and we felt that including this example in the book would increase the value and interest for our readers. It is worthwhile to note that this data set is evolving and just like other real-time data, we find that changes occur regularly, and data can have retrospective changes as more data is uncovered. It is worthwhile to mention that interpretation of data like this relies on experts in epidemiology to ensure that calculations are driven by the science of pandemics. The public COVID-19 data visualization from SAS took an entire team across SAS including health experts, product management, and research and development to keep this updated and extended as data changed. We encourage you to share your insights and visualization from this data set. Data and science hold the answers in keeping us all safe.

References

Gupta, Sujata. 2020. "Florence Nightingale understood the power of visualizing science." *Science News*. May 10, 2020.
https://www.sciencenews.org/article/florence-nightingale-birthday-power-visualizing-science

SAS. n.d. "SAS Visual Analytics SDK for developers." Accessed on September 7, 2020.
https://developer.sas.com/guides/visual-analytics-sdk.html

SAS. 2020. "2019 Novel Coronavirus Report Powered by SAS Viya." Accessed on September 7, 2020.
https://tbub.sas.com/COVID19/

United Nations. 2020. "Population Division: Data." Accessed on September 7, 2020.
https://www.un.org/development/desa/pd/data-landing-page

World Bank. 2020. "World Development Indicators." Accessed on September 7, 2020.
https://datacatalog.worldbank.org/dataset/world-development-indicators

Chapter 13: Sharing and Collaboration

Overview

How you intend to share or deploy your visualizations can greatly impact how you build them. Considering what options are available will save time in the entire process. Thinking about how your audience will consume your creations provides a clear roadmap for the analyst. This chapter will highlight the options that you have to share and consume your data visualization.

Audience

Anyone who is creating reports, dashboards, or infographics with SAS Visual Analytics, and any SAS Visual Analytics administrators, will see the possibilities of how the audience consumes the information. Managers will also learn about the options that they can ask for when interacting with their analytics teams or designing their next project. Last, but definitely not least, the audience can read this and understand their own options and what to ask for when they deal with the analytics team.

> *"The drawing shows me at a glance what would be spread over ten pages in a book."*

> *Ivan Turgenev*

Introduction

The book so far has outlined many options and features for the analyst. This chapter is focused on the sharing and collaboration options available because the audience is so important in how effective your data visualization is. This is a dedicated chapter to look at the Three Is of Visualization Value model from the audience perspective entirely.

Audience Requirements Are Critical

Before creating anything, you need to stop and ask yourself the following question: "How will this data visualization be used?" The answer to this question will guide your efforts from the start and provide you a better understanding of how much work is required. The following are some of the answers to this question. Will your project be used as any of the following?

- Printed or poster snapshot (a single point in time)
- Presentation purpose (one use only)
- Production Report (regularly updated)
- Live real-time view of the data (operations support)
- Resource for staff in the field (primarily mobile)
- Embedded application element (not for SAS users)
- Stand-alone application (a data application)

You can see from this list that there are more than enough end points for your data visualization. The challenge is easy when you only need one of these – it is then simple to work within the parameters. Often, though, you need many of these visualizations from one creation. For example, you need your data visualization for a presentation and also embedded in a web page. You get the idea – one data visualization is often asked to be all things to all audiences. The great news is that SAS Visual Analytics is extremely flexible to cater for these multiple use cases. Of course, it is always better when you consider a use case up front, and not after you finish your development processes.

We will now step through some of the available channels that SAS Visual Analytics can provide for the audience to consume your creations. We will highlight considerations and challenges to help you navigate these different channels.

Three-I Model from the Audience Perspective

If you think about the Three Is of Visualization Value model, the audience at the top of eye metaphor has many requirements to ensure that they get the most impact from the data visualizations that have been created. One key element of the experience for the audience is the interface that they use to consume the data visualization. Gone are the days where the audience was forced to enter the application dedicated to consume the data. Data is now ubiquitous and must be inserted in the world where the audience lives. This means that the application used to create cannot be the only way to interact with the data visualization.

SAS is open in new ways, and part of this openness is the increased ease to share your creations in other entry points where the audience already exists. This chapter will step through some of these examples and provide ideas for your teams to share your data visualizations or elements of your reports with your audience. Your stakeholders will appreciate that they do not have to exit their core tools to leverage the engaging data visualizations that you have created.

INFORM

AUGMENT

This step places the audience in an analyst role because they are expected to generate some additional value themselves. The audience can leverage features like the calculations in SAS Visual Analytics and introduce their own data when required.

In this step, the audience can also load a spreadsheet and simply link the new data with the existing data in SAS Viya. For more on self-service data loading, refer to Chapter 8.

Figure 13.1: Data augmentation within SAS Visual Analytics using the Data pane options

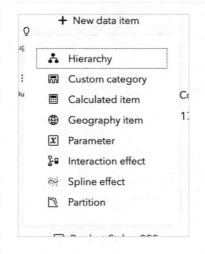

As you can see in Figure 13.1, the audience can augment data with calculations, additional data sets, and views, all within SAS Visual Analytics. This allows the audience to extend the analyst's reports with simple drag-and-drop options. Creating calculations for each row of data or as an aggregate is easy within SAS Visual Analytics using the Data pane.

PIVOT

As we progress to this step, the audience has even more simple drag-and-drop options to enhance their value from the report. Many business users are familiar with pivot tables in spreadsheets, and similar outcomes can be achieved in SAS Visual Analytics using audience-friendly options in the Data pane like the following:

- **Custom Category** – Using the custom category feature, the audience can change the automatic aggregation by introducing data groups that were not in the original data set. For example, you may want to compare your country versus the rest of the world. You can simply create a custom category and with a few mouse clicks provide this comparison without any coding or data preparation.

- **Change Measure Aggregation** – This is often overlooked as a capability for the audience. You can do this simply within SAS Visual Analytics by selecting an existing measure and changing the default aggregation whenever it is used. You could also duplicate the measure first and create alternate summarization options for different data visualizations in the report. You can try some powerful aggregations here for statistical analysis as seen in Figure 13.2.

Figure 13.2: Aggregation settings in SAS Visual Analytics

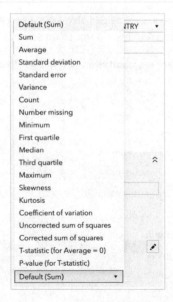

- **Duplicate Data Item** – Create your own role-playing data items. For example, if you have a date item in your data, you can create a specific aggregation or format for your final use. This is simple with a few actions as seen in Figure 13.3.

Figure 13.3: Duplicate a data item in SAS Visual Analytics

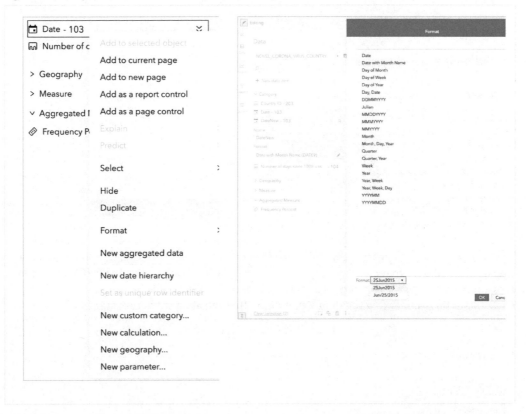

We can also consider leveraging the creation of a date hierarchy that does multiple date slices in one action as seen in Figure 13.4. This is a great way to enrich your analysis and add interactivity to your data visualizations automatically.

Figure 13.4: Simple creation of a date hierarchy

As you have a read throughout, the preceding steps in the Three Is of Visualization Value model require the audience to do work that might have been better done by the analyst. As we move forward from here, we step more into the traditional role of the audience where they are really consuming and experiencing the data visualization that the analyst has provided.

INSIGHT

CUSTOMIZE

Now we move to simpler options once more, and this places the audience in familiar territory in a consumer role. We can still enable powerful options for these users without changing the report itself or surfacing data issues or challenges. Allowing settings for the audience to do some additional analysis is a great option. The combination of View and Edit modes in SAS Visual Analytics has enabled the new power consumer mode that enables increased self-service within the framework. Options like adding data filters and elements that normally a consumer would not have access to are available.

Using the report viewing customizations, the analyst can unlock powerful self-service features for the audience using the Options pane. See an example of the customizations in Figure 13.5. These capability levels can be adjusted in the report options panel.

Figure 13.5: Viewer Customization settings within SAS Visual Analytics

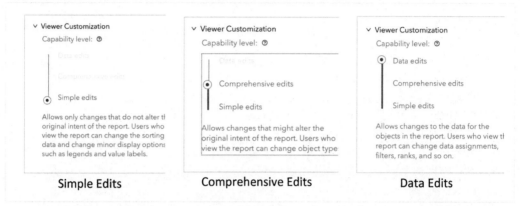

This feature unlocks simpler customization for the audience while viewing the reports created from the analyst and enables the single visualization to be reusable across many scenarios. These capabilities are important to increase the impact and value from your data visualizations within your enterprise.

CURATE

At the center of the curation step are the collaboration elements of SAS Visual Analytics. Your audience has options to be active participants in your visualizations, not just view and consume them. Providing even more control and personalization for the audience, the following two key features help enable curation of the dashboards and reports:

- **Save a Copy** – The "Save a copy" feature is available when viewing a visualization in SAS Visual Analytics. It provides the audience with the ability to save their data visualization preferences or filters for a fast start the next time they use the report.

- **Comments** – Comments are only available when viewing a report in SAS Visual Analytics. The individual viewers can provide comments at multiple levels of the report, and the team can share ideas and documents directly into the report. This provides real-time interactions and collaboration with the entire team.

These features can be seen in Figure 13.6 and provide simple, yet powerful audience options to curate within the report. Collaboration is key in this phase where analyst and audience are connecting and iterating regularly.

Figure 13.6: Collaborate with SAS Visual Analytics

TIP: SAS Drive

Collaboration is at the core of SAS Viya, and the SAS Drive application provides a centralized hub for all SAS projects and supporting files. This is leveraged in SAS Visual Analytics and other SAS solutions on SAS Viya. You can think of SAS Drive as a cloud folder storage with many interactive and interconnected features.

For more information about how to leverage SAS Drive refer to the video tutorial "Accessing Content in SAS® Drive" that is available on the SAS website.

INSPIRE

CONSUME

Visualization consumption options are where most data visualizations shine for the audience. Later in this chapter, we step through these options in much greater detail. Traditionally, consuming visualizations has been the sweet spot for the audience. You will see, however, that the world has changed, and we need to think of visualization consumption as much broader today. Here are some of the options available within SAS Viya:

- **SAS Visual Analytics** – leverage the same tools that you used to create your data visualization to also consume them.

- **Email or Text Message** – many users consume information via email or messages on social platforms and rarely depart from these productivity tools in their daily tasks.

- **SAS Add-In for Microsoft Office** – extending the productivity paradigm into the modern tools today requires direct connection to the data and the data visualization.

- **SAS Visual Analytics App** – native applications are available for mobile and tablet users to consume and interact with their visualizations.

- **SAS Visual Analytics SDK** – crafting stories are even simpler allowing for consumption of data visualizations within web pages and intranet sites.

- **Extensible Public SAS Viya APIs** – ultimate flexibility by creating alternate user interfaces to surface your data visualizations.

More details are provided in this chapter on these options.

ACT

The ultimate inspiration for the audience is delivered when you place the visualization elements directly in context with the action that the audience members need to take. Immediate impact can be achieved when we create engaging infofragments, infographics, or any data visualization. In addition, we can link to the action that we want the audience to take from this information and leverage the marketing concept of call to action (CTA). A clear CTA creates a great entry point for the rest of the data journey to continue beyond the data visualization. As seen in Figure 13.7, this is achieved by adding a link from your main network graph to an external website destination (for example, twitter.com) allowing the audience to explore a Twitter user's profile page.

Figure 13.7: Create a link from your graphs to an external website in SAS Visual Analytics

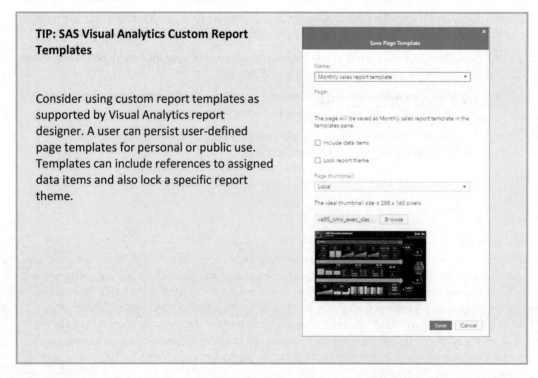

In this example, the audience can see the user name in the network graph and act on the insight right away with a single action. You can link and pass context to the destination with one or more data elements to land in the exact location desired.

Next, we dive further into the consumption options for your visualizations and look at traditional and modern ways to share your creations with the audience.

TIP: SAS Visual Analytics Custom Report Templates

Consider using custom report templates as supported by Visual Analytics report designer. A user can persist user-defined page templates for personal or public use. Templates can include references to assigned data items and also lock a specific report theme.

Consider How You Will Share Your Visualization

We have designed each of the examples in this book with the audience in mind from the beginning. The more precise the layout requirements are, the more we needed to consider how we will render these examples for the audience. For example, if you are designing a one-time use analysis or presentation image for a static infographic, then you are often the analyst and the audience simultaneously. You are going to take a screenshot of your final output and share the static image. This is less common in enterprise data visualizations, so the question always arises – will it look the same as I designed it when viewed by the audience? The short answer is that you need to consider how users will mostly interact with your report design. Are you designing for mobile devices? Are you designing for a web page? Often you want to design once and not lock yourself into any decision about the delivery platform for your design. Design once, use many. The good news is that SAS Visual Analytics is designed as a platform to achieve this exact scenario.

Like a modern data visualization platform should, SAS Visual Analytics is optimized to display on mobile devices and tablets when using these modes and adapts when on a desktop browser. This adaptive layout is great for the *design once, use many* principle. However, if you have a particular viewer in mind, then you too can optimize your design for that viewer's unique viewing experience. When creating highly formatted designs, understanding how your design will render is important to know which options are the best for your use case.

Let's step through some consumer options available when using SAS Visual Analytics.

SAS Visual Analytics

SAS provides this default interface for users to access and interact with the visualizations via a web browser, and this provides many features in addition to just viewing a data visualization, including collaboration, sharing, printing and much more. SAS Visual Analytics provides you with the ability to design, edit, and view reports in a single toolset as seen in Figure 13.8.

SAS Visual Analytics has some excellent options to increase your viewing audience across the enterprise. For example, consider using the built-in guest access option, similar to a public access mode, that provides robust settings to share data visualizations directly to the public or to the entire organization's intranet without requiring users to authenticate individually.

Consider setting a fixed report size in Edit mode of your data visualization on the report level properties. This fixes the size of the report when viewed across devices and screens. It is a great option for the small, large, tall, or wide data visualizations that you are creating if you want to control how the audience experiences the final output.

Figure 13.8: SAS Visual Analytics provides built-in viewer capabilities

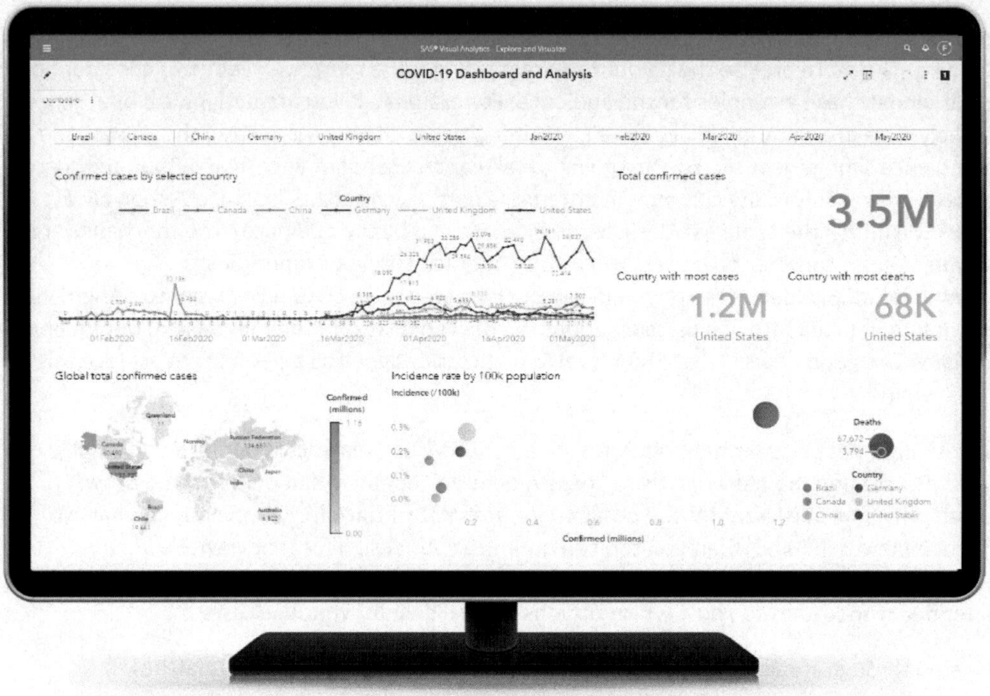

Email or Text Message

Think literally about the story your data visualization tells and look to include summary data and a narrative directly in your message. This will also include a link to data visualization and can be the best way to share the key insights with your audience without taking them away from their trusted collaboration tools. Look to leverage distribution lists or subscribe to alerts for email or text.

To enhance your emails, you might want to try the summary feature in SAS Visual Analytics to elevate your communication. The summary in your SAS Visual Analytics report can dynamically evaluate the latest data values. Leverage the summary feature for your report by creating a literal story within your project. This simple addition to your report project is enabled by default inside the report view, in emails when report is distributed, and in SAS Drive to create the headlines that matter from your data. When you have a headline to share or a data story to write, think of the summary feature to help your story have maximum impact as seen in Figure 13.9.

Figure 13.9: SAS Visual Analytics Summary creates a dynamic narrative from your data

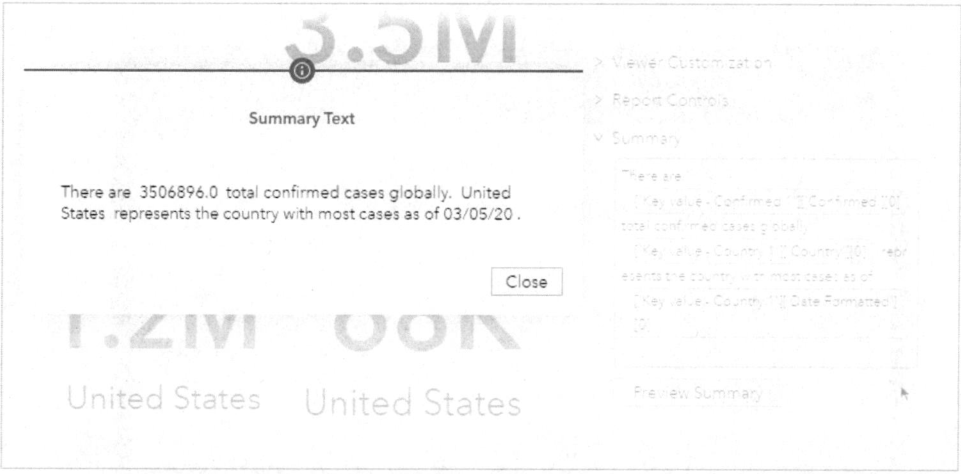

SAS Add-In for Microsoft Office

Many users can benefit from using SAS Visual Analytics reports inside Microsoft Office, and there are many features and benefits beyond just viewing the reports within this popular productivity suite using Word, PowerPoint, Excel, or Outlook. The SAS Add-In for Microsoft Office is great for embedding data-driven elements and data visualization into Office documents and presentations (Figure 13.10). We have found this is a great option for executive stakeholders to create presentations from one or more reports and remain connected to the data for the next meeting presentation.

Figure 13.10: Guided self-service BI using SAS Add-In for Microsoft Office

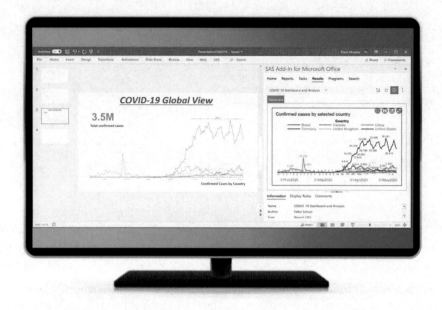

SAS Visual Analytics App

Mobile devices are the most popular way to consume information today and this extends to all users in the professional world without exception. SAS Visual Analytics reports can be used on mobile devices with only a web browser. However, the SAS Visual Analytics App, which is available for iOS, Android and Windows devices, is another great option. The SAS Visual Analytics App for iOS is the best option if you are concerned about providing accessible reports to users of your reports. There are some great features included above and beyond just viewing the reports like enhanced security, accessibility, and offline data access to name a few. The app is optimized and adaptive for all screen sizes as seen in Figure 13.11.

Figure 13.11: SAS Visual Analytics app for use on mobile and tablets

SAS Visual Analytics SDK

A software development kit is provided with SAS Visual Analytics to create custom interfaces to the data visualization. This approach is leveraged in many situations and allows organizations to create simple to complex custom data applications powered by SAS Viya directly.

Figure 13.12: SAS Visual Analytics SDK with embedded COVID-19 data visualization

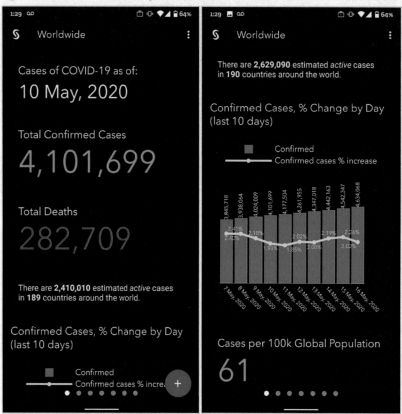

As seen in Figure 13.12, you see an image of the SAS COVID-19 data visualization being surfaced inside a custom mobile application using the SAS Visual Analytics SDK. You can view the visualizations in the report or a custom application like this.

SAS has created the SAS Visual Analytics SDK with many included features to provide fast embedding and sharing of SAS Visual Analytics reports in external applications and web pages. This means that a lightweight version of the report or graph is generated on load and can be used to place into a web page or called by another web service. This can be seen in Figure 13.13 where the copy link feature on a report or report object can generate a request to SAS Visual Analytics SDK via simple drag-and-drop options.

Figure 13.13: Embedding and sharing reports and report objects

Using the "copy link" feature enables analysts to embed custom objects from SAS Visual Analytics into other web applications without coding. This not only lets you include the entire report but also selected pages or tabs, a single graph or container, and the contents as seen in Figure 13.14. The public COVID-19 data visualization from SAS leverages this SDK and the underlying SAS Visual Analytics report objects to call the data visualization elements directly from a standard web page.

Figure 13.14: SAS Visual Analytics SDK embedded into a web page

Figure 13.15: Sample SAS Visual Analytics SDK elements embedded into a web page (source code view)

```
</nav>
<div id="main" class="container">
    <h1>2019 Novel Coronavirus</h1>
    <p>In December 2019, a new respiratory disease was discovered in Wuhan, China. The
    illness is caused by a new type of coronavirus, known as "severe acute respiratory
    syndrome coronavirus 2," or SARS-CoV-2. The illness that can result from this virus
    infection is called "coronavirus disease 2019," or COVID-19. On March 11, 2020 - <a
    href="https://www.who.int/emergencies/diseases/novel-coronavirus-2019"> WHO </a> declared
    the outbreak a global pandemic. This report uses SAS® Viya to visualize metrics and
    trends related to the COVID-19 pandemic.
    </p>
    <!-- <div class="text-center mt-5"><p>Cases as of:</p></div> -->
    <div class="d-flex justify-content-center"><sas-report-object objectName="ve48825"
    authenticationType="guest" url="https://tbub.sas.com"
    reportUri="/reports/reports/f69dd29c-8ed6-4201-97fa-ae29a7fd8c01" style="width:400px;">
    </sas-report-object>
    </div>
```

As Figure 13.15 shows, only a simple HTML tag *<sas-report-object/>* is required to embed your data visualization into a web page. You can learn more about supported tags as well as attributes in the SAS Visual Analytics SDK example and developer documentation. This opens a world of possibility for creating data journeys for your audience. The SDK is simple and flexible. You can embed many levels of the report using the built-in generated links and of course extend this with the SAS Visual Analytics SDK for SAS Viya. It all starts with a simple action: *copy link*.

Extensible Public SAS Viya APIs

The documented public API for creating flexible consumption options like embedding SAS Visual Analytics objects in your business applications or custom web/mobile applications is provided to allow endless entry points into SAS Viya. The API options are built into the GUI to show a common use case; however, applications can also be coded by a developer and will unlock many entry points into your SAS Viya solution. We like to think of this as a create once and use anywhere approach with SAS Visual Analytics as the data visualization engine. We can share and innovate together at developer.sas.com, which includes examples and documentation to make SAS Visual Analytics work for your needs.

You can create your own applications that leverage SAS Visual Analytics too. This could include applications that integrate with SAS Viya on a compute or data-level only, and the resultant data can drive your applications. You can also leverage a combination of data visualization elements from your reports to other non-SAS elements of an application. As seen in Figure 13.16, we could have built a poster-sized version of the data visualization with all the features that we wanted. However, we can use the report image viewer API included in SAS Visual Analytics and an open-source custom Scalable Vector Graphic (SVG) Viewer to display the first *N* pages of a report as an infographic poster – just like magic (Schulz and Murphy 2018)! This example creates a live SVG image of each of the first three report pages and displays them in an alternative viewer – the SVG Viewer custom app that we created as a demonstration of this capability. This app allows the user to navigate and zoom in and out, leveraging crystal-clear SVG images dynamically generated by SAS Visual Analytics. This is an example of how open SAS Viya is for innovative data projects.

Figure 13.16: Example custom SVG viewer developed with documented APIs and open source

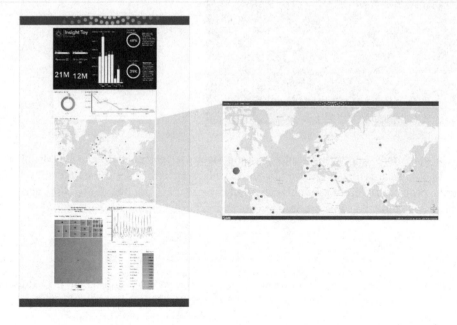

TIP: The Importance of Accessibility

Accessibility is a key part of consuming your reports, and SAS has built-in accessibility options via the SAS Graphics Accelerator. This is a free Google Chrome extension that enables users with visual impairments or blindness to explore data visualizations. It supports alternative presentations of data visualizations that include enhanced visual rendering, text descriptions, tabular data, and interactive sonification. Sonification uses non-speech audio to convey important information about the graph. This powerful feature can make your SAS Visual Analytics reports ready for all audience requirements. For more information about creating accessible reports, see *Creating Accessible Reports with SAS Visual Analytics*.

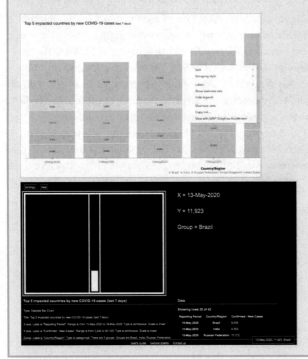

There are always more ways to share and consume the powerful analytics from SAS Visual Analytics, and these are some of the options we have leveraged to share our own data visualization projects. Different channels can often cater to many additional use cases and scenarios, and we outlined some of these to explain the flexibility that they provide.

Conclusion

This chapter was a dedicated look at how the audience interacts with reports and the value that they get from those interactions. We spent some time stepping through the consumption options for impactful data visualizations and how you can place the data visualization content directly into the daily life of your audience. This approach brings the visualization to the audience, rather than bringing the audience to the visualization. Extending the standard entry points and creating specific journeys for your audience is the expectation of the modern enterprise. Design visualizations once and use many places is a great way to think of SAS Visual Analytics. Do not be limited in your ideas to get more audience eyes on your creations. The interconnected modern world is providing more and more integration options for data visualization, and we encourage you to keep striving to improve the audience experience with your SAS Visual Analytics projects.

References

Bizoux, Xavier. 2019. "SAS Visual Analytics Report Summary, what kind of beast is this?" SAS Communities, April 23, 2019. https://communities.sas.com/t5/SAS-Communities-Library/SAS-Visual-Analytics-Report-Summary-what-kind-of-beast-is-this/ta-p/553138 .

Murphy, Travis and Schulz, Falko. 2018. "Supercharge Your Dashboards with Infographic Concepts Using SAS® Visual Analytics," In Proceedings of the SAS® Global Forum 2018 Conference. Cary, NC: SAS Institute Inc. https://www.sas.com/content/dam/SAS/support/en/sas-global-forum-proceedings/2018/2069-2018.pdf

SAS. n.d. "Accessing Content in SAS® Drive," Accessed May 1, 2020. https://video.sas.com/detail/video/5808938115001/accessing-content-in-sas%C2%AE-drive.

SAS. n.d. "SAS® Visual Analytics SDK," Accessed August 1, 2020. https://developer.sas.com/sdk/va/.

SAS. 2020. "Creating Accessible Reports with SAS Visual Analytics 8.5," SAS.com last updated June 12, 2020. https://documentation.sas.com/?cdcId=vacdc&cdcVersion=8.5&docsetId=vacar&docsetTarget=titlepage.htm

Turgenev, Ivan. 1862. *Fathers and Children,* trans. Constance Garnett. New York: P.F. Collier & Son, 1917. http://www.gutenberg.org/files/30723/30723-h/30723-h.htm

Chapter 14: Future of Data Visualization

Overview

In this chapter, we look at planning where to go from here and highlight that the learning continues and that software is forever changing. It is the reader's challenge to stay informed and aware of the latest changes in SAS software. This last chapter sets a vision for emerging trends and potential tools and technologies to influence the next generation of data dashboards. As SAS continues to innovate in data visualization and analytics with regular updates to the software offerings used in this book, more power is being introduced in this area all the time.

Audience

This final chapter is for all SAS users as we attempt to outline a future for data visualization projects and summarize the book.

> *"In ten years, we expect to remember every song we ever heard, recall every person we ever met, and transact with everyone, regardless of the language they speak."*

Oliver Schabenberger

Introduction

When we started this book project, we discussed using many terms like "dashboard" and were looking at "data visualization," "information journey," or "data journey" and many more, as we believe that the term dashboard has been around for so long. What we realized was that many teams looking at creating innovation with data often asked for a data visualization as one of the core and central deliverables. Then we researched what the start-up data visualization companies were calling their equivalent outputs, and dashboard kept on coming up again and again. So, we decided to use the data visualization term and use this as an anchor throughout this book. We will spend some time looking into the future to see what it may hold for data visualization.

Future Trends

We understand that many of you have your own ideas on what the future can hold, and this section allows us to share our ideas with you all. We understand that this is a tough task in the world today with innovations hiding around every corner and digital disruption continuing to impact industries across the globe. That said, we will provide our ideas below. The following are our top emerging trends for the next five years in data visualization and analytics.

Figure 14.1: Virtual reality prototype application for analyzing SAS Viya network graphs (Schulz and Marković 2019)

New Entry Points – Technology Innovation

Channels and delivery continue to change each day. The rise of new collaboration tools and trendsetting social media applications requires data visualization to evolve also. With the rise of wearables including watches, always-on headphones, and heads up display glasses (Augmented and Virtual Reality), we can see that the options require big data to support them, so the dashboards need to be ready for these new channels also. Figure 14.1 shows a sample of what this might look like from the 2019 SAS Global Forum paper "The Infinite Canvas: Analyzing Social Networks in Virtual Space" (Schulz and Marković 2019).

Art Merged with Science

Design and data will become more connected in the next five years, and businesses cannot just talk about being data-driven. Organizations will use data visualization to inform all elements of business operations. There will be no more excuses. Artificial intelligence (AI) will enable the connection from artistic to scientific, creating more impact with much less effort. The bridge between AI and humans will continue to be visual triggers or other sensory triggers. Data visualization provides rapid context to support natural language alerts supporting rapid decision making. In the future, you could see our three-I model being automated with AI to assist at each stage, making the skills gap less and less over coming years.

Crowd Sourcing Data Visualization

The collective is a powerful concept that drives SAS and is part of our DNA. The work during the COVID-19 pandemic has highlighted this again, and initiatives like Data4Good and data volunteerism continue to rise. Collaboration will continue into the future and will open up many new solutions for benefiting humanity. Check the SAS GatherIQ site to get involved (SAS 2020).

Data Visualization Literacy

What are considered complex graphs and visualizations today will become mainstream tomorrow. This might take some time; however, the literacy of the audience will continue to develop, allowing the depth of the visuals to expand. Network analysis displayed on maps or statistical composite graphs to show performance of AI models will all be mainstream in the near future. SAS Viya enables AI projects today, and this includes democratized AI with graphs and visuals. This will continue and start to spread toward the audience using these interfaces, not just data scientists.

Beyond Dashboards

If you look at the evolution of data and the intersection of data into our lives via technology and digital transformation, you quickly see that everything starts to behave like a dashboard. The term dashboard will probably come and go and, as we have observed, it may sit under the surface for the traditional data teams to refer to. In reality, these are just data applications that are the front door to the next generation AI data projects of tomorrow.

Talk to ME!

Learning from your previous usage and complimentary profile comparisons, the data visualization will automatically display context just for you. No more clicks or instructions needed. This hyper personalization is seen in many industries across the globe, and data visualization will continue this direction. For the analyst, this means that one data visualization will be rendered for the individual context automatically, which minimizes the effort needed to create impact. Your preferences and behavior will determine how data is highlighted or displayed.

Big Data Visualization

Data visualization must be scalable as data becomes ubiquitous and everything is big data. The data visualization platform needs to include the next wave of compute options and algorithms. Scalable data visualization is just a requirement moving forward.

Technology Landscape

Consolidation of technology vendors has continued in recent years with investments from Salesforce and Google in data visualization acquisitions and many more consolidations and partnerships. This is what occurred in the business intelligence world, and now is looking like the next start-ups will be merged with larger tech companies who see the value in this user experience with data. This new wave of acquisitions shows that the data visualization segment of data and analytics is hotter than ever.

Open for Business

Open will not be optional anymore. Your data project needs to move seamlessly from technology to technology. This is in the visuals tier and algorithm tier. SAS has made great steps to achieve this open ecosystem, and this will continue as an important element in the years to come.

Conversations with Data

Natural language processing (NLP) and natural language generation (NLG) will continue to grow and finally step out from the novelty phase to human-like interactions. The AI embedded in SAS Viya will continue to be applied to SAS solutions and combining visuals with language to leap directly from question to context and shorten the time to understanding to a fraction of today.

Audience and Analyst

Let's take a moment to recap the Three Is of Visualization Value model from our book and link it to the future of data visualization. Remember that visualization value is often limited by the software features, the skills of the author, and the skills of the audience. This can define how much value the data visualization will provide. Does the project **Inform**, provide **Insight**, or **Inspire**?

As you can see in Figure 14.2, the Three Is of Visualization Value model overlays the audience and analyst skills onto the value scale to show what can occur if we forget who we are creating the data journey for. Thinking of the audience right from the start, the analyst can create the correct value from their projects.

Figure 14.2: The Three Is of Visualization Value

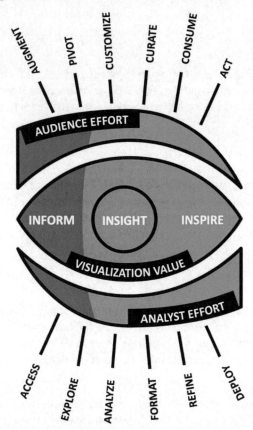

Based around our predictions on the future trends in data visualization, we can see that potential artificial intelligence may reduce the skills gap between audience and analyst and augment some of these steps. However, we are many years away from replacement by robots when it comes to complete end-to-end data analysis and storytelling. So, we should continue to leverage the improvements in the software tools and continue the investment into our own training and skills to ensure we are ready for all data journeys in our future.

Next Steps

This book provides starting points and ideas for your data visualization projects; however, there are not enough pages to cover all ideas and approaches. We included references and further reading in each chapter to enable some additional options for continuing your learning. To keep up with all the new features and options, keep connected to SAS social media and the content on SAS.com, which is always fresh and updated. We encourage you to connect with the communities.sas.com service also, which provides instant collaboration with SAS users across the globe. You will find that the authors of this book post regularly.

Of course, once you master these free channels for learning SAS, you can take your skills to the next level with online and classroom training programs from SAS or leverage SAS certification programs to really know the software and all it offers you and your business. When you are starting your next data project, remember to ask if your team is leveraging all the options within SAS Viya.

Conclusion

Here is a final comment on this book and the goals that we aimed to achieve when we set out writing it.

The aim of this book is to show how SAS Visual Analytics can be leveraged for creating impactful dashboards for a better user experience. We hope that this book has provided some ideas about how you can adopt and achieve data-driven visualization in your business. We hope that our step-by-step guides to create impactful dashboards with SAS provides some ideas and helps you put these ideas into action. We encourage you to share your creations and experiences on the SAS Visual Analytics gallery at communities.sas.com.

Remember that data visualization can answer many questions, and if you always consider the audience, you will be creating the correct entry point to keep them coming back for more. We also spent some time highlighting how SAS is key when considering data visualization because the analytics life cycle needs more than just pretty graphs. Your enterprise deserves more from your chosen software user interface. This book leverages the power of big data and the SAS analytics engine and places this in your users lives to interact with every day. Thanks for taking the time to come down this path with us. Let's keep on telling these stories with data and take advantage of the breadth and depth of features using SAS Visual Analytics on SAS Viya. In closing, we thank you for spending your valuable time with us and exploring our little book. We appreciate you.

References

SAS Institute Inc. n.d. "SAS Training," Accessed August 1, 2020 https://www.sas.com/en_ae/training/overview.html. SAS Institute Inc. n.d. "GatherIQApp| SAS," Accessed August 1, 2020. https://gatheriq.analytics/.

Schabenberger, Oliver. 2018. "Five Trends That Are Going To Shape Future Of Tech." *Business World*, May 7, 2018. http://www.businessworld.in/article/Five-Trends-That-Are-Going-To-Shape-Future-Of-Tech/07-05-2018-148443/.

Schulz, Falko and Marković, Nikola. 2019. "The Infinite Canvas: Analyzing Social Networks in Virtual Space." In Proceedings of the SAS® Global Forum 2019 Conference. Cary, NC: SAS Institute Inc. https://www.sas.com/content/dam/SAS/support/en/sas-global-forum-proceedings/2019/3364-2019.pdf.

Ready to take your SAS® and JMP® skills up a notch?

Be among the first to know about new books,
special events, and exclusive discounts.
support.sas.com/newbooks

Share your expertise. Write a book with SAS.
support.sas.com/publish

sas.com/books
for additional books and resources.

THE POWER TO KNOW.